The Etiquette Advantage®

SociallySmart™Skills for Personal Success

Other Books by Jane Hight McMurry

The Dance Steps of Life™
Readers Theatre for Senior Citizens
Success is a Team Effort

The Etiquette Advantage®

SociallySmart™ Skills For Personal Success

Jane Hight McMurry

Stellar Publishing

FIRST EDITION 2002

Library of Congress Cataloging-in-Publication Data

McMurry, Jane Hight.
  The Etiquette Advantage®/Jane Hight McMurry.
    Includes bibliographical references.
    ISBN 0970304137
    1. Etiquette
    2. Social Skills
    3. Interpersonal Communication
    4. Character Development
        I. McMurry, Jane Hight. II. Title.

Library of Congress Control Number: 2001129356 (alk.paper)

Summary: Explains personal social skills and manners that lead to success.

Printed in the United States of America

Book Design by Debra Hobbs

In Thanksgiving for My Family

For my parents,
Joan Williams Hight and Henry Wesley Hight, who provided
a loving, supportive environment enabling me to develop a
positive self-concept, the strength of my convictions, and the
courage to express them.

For my brother,
"Chip," Henry Wesley Hight, Jr., a beacon of integrity.

For my husband,
Gene, whose sterling qualities inspire me.

And for my daughters,
Winifred Joan and Allison Louise, two irreplaceable gifts.

SociallySmart™ speaker, author, and trainer Jane Hight McMurry is the president of *Socially Smart*™and founder and managing director of **The Etiquette Advantage**® which provides training and support resources to help people achieve *Socially Smart*™ skills in communicating with people for professional and personal success. She is the author of *The Dance Steps of Life*™, *The Etiquette Advantage*®, *Readers Theatre for Senior Citizens*, and co-author of *Success is a Team Effort*. Jane speaks to audiences at all levels, from the frontline to the boardroom that want to achieve excellence in communicating with people.

CONTENTS

TO THE READER

Dear Readers,

Etiquette is a useful tool which opens doors. In fact, originally it was a ticket proving that the bearer knew the rules required for admittance behind closed doors. Today etiquette continues to open doors for those lucky enough to possess it. The mission of *The Etiquette Advantage®* is to unlock the secrets of social success.

Knowledge of social skills does not guarantee that all doors will open or guarantee achievement of personal and career goals such as a spot in a select college or a seat in an executive boardroom. However, it is likely that the doors to many rooms will likely be closed for those who lack these skills.

Different types of etiquette exist in North American culture including social, business, and service etiquette (military protocol). The focus of this book is on basic social etiquette in North America. The purpose of this book is to serve as a general guide to the customs and courtesies in North America. However, where it seems natural and appropriate, information is given to the reader to prepare him for basic interaction with people practicing business etiquette and military protocol.

The customs of social etiquette in North America often vary in different regions. In fact, the customs within a community may differ between different groups. Religious and ethnic traditions are often the reason for these differences. One custom is no better than another is –it is simply different. A courteous person endeavors to be aware of differences and to treat those customs with respect.

Jane Hight McMurry
Socially Smart™
President and Founder,
The Etiquette Advantage®

MEETING AND GREETING

SMILE: The number one way to make others feel good is to smile while looking at them. Smiling puts others at ease and shows you are interested in them. In addition, it releases tension. Did you know it takes fewer muscles to smile than to frown? Forget about your problems and show you care about others by flashing your pearly whites. Out of shape, flabby, frowning facial muscles can be whipped into shape with practice. Pull out the mirror and practice pulling up your smile.

EYE CONTACT: Look people in the face when you greet them. Looking at them develops a sense of trust and shows that you're interested in them. You and the other person will feel more comfortable if you avoid staring into their eyes for a long time. Practice this exercise for maximum comfort the next time you are meeting with someone: Look at the person's total face for five seconds. Then look at each part of the person's face for a few seconds (eyes, nose, forehead, chin, and hair).

SHAKING HANDS: Shake hands firmly with people you greet. Shake hands using your right hand and remember to clasp hands "web to web." A weak, mousy, limp shake is called a fish shake. Some people interpret this handshaker as wimpy and lacking self-confidence. The bone crushing handshaker is often interpreted as a bully. Make your shake moderately firm and shake for about three seconds.

SAYING HELLO: Greet others with a friendly "hello" and be enthusiastic. "How are you?" is an overused greeting that often sounds mechanical and evokes an even more mechanical, "Fine, how are you?" Don't ask how a person is unless you truly want to know. Positive greetings like, "It's great to meet you," "I've heard lots about you from my cousin, friend, etc.," or "I hear you play on the basketball team," are upbeat and likely will lead to conversations both of you will enjoy.

INTRODUCTIONS

Meeting and Greeting includes smiling, making eye contact, saying hello, and standing up to shake hands by both women and men. In the olden days, a woman stood only to meet and greet an older woman or dignitary. Further, a woman did not shake hands unless she chose to extend her hand to a man. Today, equal respect is shown to both sexes. The most important part of meeting and greeting is called the introduction.

Introductions are the way we make ourselves or our family and friends known to others. We've all been in that awkward situation when we encounter a friend who is with someone we don't know. We talk for a moment and the unknown person stands there uncomfortably. No move is made to introduce the stranger. We leave the encounter feeling unfulfilled and a bit guilty. The stranger leaves the encounter feeling unfulfilled and angry. The outward appearance is that he wasn't important enough to be acknowledged. The real reason the friend neglected to make the introduction is his feeling of insecurity about how to make a correct introduction.

How to Introduce Yourself

Stand up, look the person in the eye, extend your hand for a firm web to web handshake and say your name and something about yourself. For example,

"Hello, I'm Jane McMurry. I'm Kathy's tennis partner from Wilmington."

The key is to give as much concise information about yourself as possible in a short amount of time. This is conversation bait. Conversation bait encourages the other person to respond to the information.

"It's nice to meet you. I'm Jane's friend, Ronna Zimmer, who went with the tennis group to Camp Cathy last summer."

How to Properly Introduce Others

• Stand up and make eye contact as you are saying each person's name.

• Say the older, more important, or female's name first followed by one of the following phrases: "I'd like to present to you," "I would like to introduce to you," "I would like for you to meet," or simply, "this is" followed by the name of the person being introduced. For example, "Judy Goodman, I'd like to introduce to you my neighbor, Jim Faler."

• Make each person feel important by providing important information about each person as you make the introduction. Telling about the interests, special talents, hometowns or even the schools of the people being introduced will give a basis for small talk. For example, say, "Winston, I'd like to introduce to you to my friend from camp, Jeremiah, who is a magician from Montreal, Canada." An introduction such as this can result in several avenues of conversation – camp experience, magic, the city of Montreal and the country of Canada!

Important!

If you come upon a friend and a group of people you don't know, make the first move - introduce yourself!

Three Rules for Making Proper Social Introductions

Introduce:

- Less important persons *to* more important persons

- Men *to* women

- Younger people *to* older people (Accomplish this by saying the more important woman's, or older person's name first.)

Exceptions

- Outsiders are given precedence when being introduced to a family member. The exception is a child introducing his mother or father.

- Women are presented to ambassadors, chiefs of state, royalty and dignitaries of the church.

Example of Introducing a Parent and a Young Friend

"Mom, I'd like to introduce to you my friend, Eleanor Wilkins. Eleanor, this is my mom, Mrs. Hight, who made the homemade cookies for our trip to the coast."

"Dad, I'd like to introduce to you my friend, Pat Koonce who was in Gene's class in New Hampshire. Pat, this is my father, Mr. Hight."

Examples of Introductions to Church and Government Officials

"Bishop Daniels, I'd like to introduce to you my friend, Mary Arthur Stoudemire. She serves on the vestry at The Chapel of the Cross in Chapel Hill."

"Mr. President, may I present Worth Price, a Vice President at Allied Pharmaceutical."

Example of Introducing a Teacher and a Parent

(Even if your teacher is younger than your parents, show deference and respect to the teacher by making the teacher the most important person in the way you phrase the introduction.)

"Ms. Barry, I'd like to introduce to you my mother, Joan Hight. Mom, this is my math teacher, Ms. Barry."

Example of Family Introductions

"Elsa Desrochers, I'd like to introduce my brother, Chip Hight."

Example of Introducing Two Friends to Each Other

"Wendy Murphy, I'd like to introduce Nancy Stutzman. Wendy, I met Nancy this summer at the Outing Club. Nancy, Wendy is the friend I told you about who has the house on the lake in New Hampshire." (Provide something of interest to talk about.)

Polish your introductions by practicing the following:

- **Introduce a less important person to a more important person** if you can determine the more important person. Do this by first saying the more important person's name.
For example,

  "Mr. President, I'd like to present my uncle, Governor Nutting." Or Professor Stamey, I'd like to introduce to you my roommate from Virginia, Karen Layman."

- **Introduce a man to a woman when they are the same age.** Do this by first saying the woman's name. For example,

  "Ellen Carter, I'd like to introduce to you my godfather, Howard Allen. Howard, Ellen is my cousin from Pennsylvania."

- **Introduce a younger person to an older person.** Do this by first saying the older person's name. For example,

  "Grandmother, I'd like to introduce to you my guitar teacher, Ms. Poole. Ms. Poole, this is my grandmother from Henderson, Mrs. Hight."

- **Introduce a new friend to a group.** Do this by first saying the new friend's name. For example,

  "Dale Zimmer, I'd like you to meet my friends."
  Then say the names of the members in the group or

have your friends introduce themselves to your friend.

Rise for Introductions

Always rise for any introduction. Rising is a gesture of respect for both the person to whom you are being introduced and yourself.

Handling Honorifics

An honorific is a title such as Dr., Mr., Ms., Mrs., and Miss

- Young people use an honorific when addressing an adult unless the adult has asked the young person to call him by a familiar first name. A young person who has not been asked to call an adult by a first name begins the introduction with the adult's name preceded by the appropriate honorific. For example, the young person introducing another young person to an adult would say,

  "Mrs. Wessell, I'd like to introduce Clarence Mills."

  An honorific is normally not used for a young person in introductions. If the young person making the introduction does call the adult by a familiar name, he is correct to begin the introduction of the older person without using the honorific but he needs to include the use of the honorific during the introduction so the young person being introduced will know the correct honorific to use when addressing the adult. For example,

"Bill, I'd like to introduce my friend from the western tour, Clarence Mills. Clarence, Judge Hight used to practice law with my father."

- Correctly use the titles of people. Greet your doctor or dentist by saying "Hello, Dr. Craig." Not, "Hi, Mr. Craig."

Responding to Introductions

- Do not reply with a simple "Hi," or "Hello."

- Stand up, extend your hand, smile, lean towards the person and say, "Hello, 'David'. How do you do." Some people prefer to say the phrase "It's nice to meet you." Even though the traditional response is "How do you do," remember it's helpful if you can personalize what you say.

- Always repeat the person's name.

- Immediately ask the person to repeat a name if you didn't hear the name properly or are not sure of how to pronounce it.

Handshaking

The handshake is the accepted greeting for men and women in almost every country around the world. Even the Japanese will bow and shake hands when beginning and ending a meeting in the Western world. Don't hold back - extend your hand immediately. You are judged by your handshake. Older women were taught they should initiate the handshake. This is not so in today's world where women take their place equally beside men. (Exception: In European countries, the custom continues for a woman to offer her hand first.) A warm, sincere handshake makes a positive, tactile connection with another person.

Polite Points for Handshaking

- Be ready to initiate and receive a handshake.

- Extend your hand vertically with the thumb up and out.

- Don't curve your hand or offer only your fingertips.

- Contact should be web to web.

- Keep your hand firm with some tension. No one likes the "limp fish" handshake!

- Don't squeeze too hard.

- Shake using two smooth pumps from the elbow, not the wrist or shoulder.

- Accompany handshakes with direct eye contact and a smile!

Negative Handshakes

The Bone Crusher Handshake. This handshake exerts so much strength that it hurts the hand of the person receiving it. The person giving this handshake is sending the message that he is aggressive, angry, insecure and/or intimidating.

The Fingertip Extender. Many women were taught to offer only their fingertips when shaking hands. This weak, unsatisfying handshake sends the message that the person offering this handshake lacks self-confidence and wishes to keep other people at a distance.

The Gloved Handshake. Sometimes referred to as the "preacher" handshake, this handshake conveys the message of comfort and consolation. The gloved handshake is given by shaking hands with the right hand and then placing the left hand on top of the clasped hands. It is best used with close friends or when conveying sympathy or offering comfort. The gloved handshake should not be used as an everyday greeting.

The Limp Fish. A handshake with no tension or tone in the hand feels weak and lifeless. A negative impression is formed instantly when a limp fish handshake is given.

Handshaking Hindrances

- If you are prone to clammy or perspiring hands, carry a handkerchief or small powder puff in your pocket. Squeeze it to discreetly absorb perspiration. Or use antiperspirant on your hands 24 hours before an event. A prescription medication called drysol is also available for excessive hand perspiration.

- If your hands are dirty, wipe them off if possible. If not, simply say something like, "I'd like to shake hands, but ... I've been working in the yard and my hands are dirty."

- Rings can be painful when shaking hands—it's best not to wear them on the right hand.

- It is correct for either a man or woman to initiate a handshake. However, no one should refuse or ignore an outstretched hand.

Shake Hands When

- Making introductions.

- Saying hello or good bye.

- Greeting someone who comes to your home and when bidding farewell.

- Congratulating or consoling.

- Entering or leaving a room.

How to Handle Disabilities and Handshaking

It's appropriate to shake hands or touch a person who has a disability. The impression you make will be positive as disabled individuals appreciate the same gestures of courtesy and respect extended to anyone else. Make an effort to reach out and touch the person without missing a beat.

- If the person has an artificial limb, it's okay to touch his upper arm or the prosthesis in greeting.

- The person may extend the other hand. Senator Robert Dole shakes with his left hand because his right one is withered from a combat injury.

- Even if the person is paralyzed, you may squeeze his arm or hand.

- When greeting a blind person you may say, "I'd like to shake your hand" and wait for the person to offer his hand.

"Life is not so short but that there is always time enough for courtesy."

Ralph Waldo Emerson

WHEN TO STAND

All Stand for Introductions

Modern manners encourage women and men to rise for all introductions. Standing to meet someone is a gesture of self-respect and respect to those in attendance.

Note to women: In earlier days, older women did not stand when a man or younger woman was introduced. Today, modern women do stand unless a physical limitation may prevent it or make the motion awkward. In addition, women did not shake hands with all they met. Today, women correctly shake hands with persons of any age as a sign of respect.

Host and Hostess Stand

Stand to greet all guests.

Family Members Stand

All family members stand when a guest enters a room in their home. Every member of the host's family should rise when a guest enters the room as well as greet the guests with a pleasant greeting, a welcoming smile, firm handshake, and good eye contact. A child sitting and already talking with an adult guest need not rise each time a guest comes into the room unless the guest is brought to him/her for an introduction. In that case, all rise for introductions.

Men Stand

• A man stands when a woman enters the room for the first time and continues to stand until the woman is seated or leaves the area.

• A man stands when a woman comes to sit by him. The man sits after the woman is seated. A man stands when a woman leaves.

Note: The man stands for every woman who enters his area and stops to talk. He does not need to rise for unknown women who are simply passing through his area. *Men make the gesture of half-rising and nodding when a passing woman greets a man dining. The man completely stands if the woman stops to talk. He does not sit until the woman sits or leaves.*

When to Rise at Home and in the Workplace

Women and men should rise when a guest enters the room. It is good manners to offer a guest a seat and to remain standing until the guest is seated. The host should stand when the guest rises to leave and remains standing as long as the guest stands and then walks the guest to the door, opens the door for the guest to leave, and may walk the guest to the door, to the elevator or building exit, or to his car. Business protocol does not require that business people rise for assistants or secretaries who frequently enter and exit the room.

RECEIVING LINES

Receiving lines are often found at formal dances, elegant parties and wedding receptions. The purpose of a receiving line is to give the hosts of a formal event an opportunity to greet each of the guests. The receiving line also provides guests with an opportunity to meet and greet guests of honor. It is good manners for a guest to go through a receiving line upon arrival at an event. Do be on time. Receiving lines traditionally last only 30-45 minutes. Find your host and apologize if you are late. Failure to go through a receiving line or to speak to your host is an unpardonable social sin. Fie!

The Formation of the Receiving Line

The formation of a receiving line is simple. The senior hostess, host, or visiting dignitary is the first person in the receiving line that presents the guest of honor who is second in line. The honored guest stands to the right of the host. The third person in the line is the host. Fourth in line is the spouse of the guest of honor. This line order gives the hosts the opportunity to introduce all other guests to the guest of honor and his/her spouse. The remaining members of the receiving line are positioned in terms of age, rank or seniority. Each receiving line member has his/her spouse by his/her side. Traditionally, a woman stands on the man's right.

How To Go Through A Receiving Line

A woman traditionally precedes her escort through a receiving line. It is correct for the woman to introduce herself. If the woman brings guests to the event, she precedes her guests and introduces them to the host who in turn introduces her and her guests to the guest of honor.

When going through the receiving line, introduce yourself to the host/hostess first. (If time and the length of the line permits, you should say how you came to attend the function, or give your relation to the guest of honor or the host/hostess or bride and groom.)

The host/hostess then shakes your hand and introduces you to the next person in the receiving line. Each person should introduce the guest to the next person in line until the guest has been introduced to everyone in the line. The person to whom you are being introduced extends his or her hand first.

Men precede women through receiving lines only if the event takes place at The White House, an all-male campus, or at a military event when he is enlisted and she is not. (If both male and female are enlisted, the lower ranking person goes through the line first. If their rank is equal, they may choose who goes first). Protocol at these places requires that the man go through the line first so he can introduce the woman.

What Hosts Say and Do in a Receiving Line

- Shake hands with all guests.

- Say something polite and introduce guests to guest of honor. For example, "Hello, Thomas. It's great to see you. This is our guest of honor, Senator Smith."

- Keep conversations brief so the line can move quickly.

- Do not eat or drink in a receiving line.

What Guests Say and Do in a Receiving Line

- Shake hands with all members in a receiving line.

- Say hello and introduce themselves if unknown to members of the receiving line.

- Briefly comment how they happen to be at the event. ("I'm the cousin of the bride.")

- Introduce their guests to the members of the receiving line.

- Keep conversations brief so the line can move quickly.

- Do not eat or drink in a receiving line.

Example of What to Say as You Go through a Receiving Line at a Party

Guest: "Good evening, my name is Allison McMurry."

Host/Hostess: "Good evening, Allison. This is our guest of honor, Kate Reece."

Example of What to Say going Through a Receiving Line at a Wedding

Guest: "Congratulations! (Said only to the groom) or Best Wishes! (Said only to the bride). I'm Jane McMurry and I'm the groom's cousin."

When greeting the parents of the bride and groom or the members of the bridal party, again, simply state your name and relationship to the bride and groom.

Etiquette for Leaving a Party or Event

Upon leaving a party or event, always thank the host/hostess and give a sincere compliment about the evening. Examples are how much the ceremony or party has been enjoyed, how beautiful the flowers/decorations are, how lovely/handsome the host/hostess look, how delicious the food was.

Always thank your host and say goodbye before you get your coat. Avoid saying goodbye to your host with your coat over your arm as this is just as bad manners as saying goodbye to your host after you've put on your coat.

CONVERSATION SKILLS

Small talk is what people say to each other to be polite. We've all felt awkward when we've met new people or when we've been at someone's home and we just didn't know what to say.

Conversing with Ease

- Take a risk – be the first to say hello.
  "Hello, I'm Fred Jones. My brother is on this team. Do you know any of the players on this lacrosse team?"

- Focus on your immediate environment.
  "What a fun party? How do you know Clara?"

- Be yourself.

- Balance the conversation – talking and listening.

- Seek out common interests and experiences.

- Ask easy-to-answer questions that let the person know you want to get to know him:
  "Do you go to Alderman School?"
  "What's your favorite sport?"
  "How many brothers and sisters do you have?"
  "Who's your computer instructor?"

- Ask open-ended questions.
  These questions usually begin with words like How? Why? In what way? How did you get involved...?

Examples:

"How did you get involved in rock climbing?"
"Why did your family choose to vacation at this resort?"
"How long have you been taking guitar lessons?"

- Answer a question with more than two words.
  "I've been taking guitar for two years – I hope to play with a band this year." Do not simply say, "Two years."

Tips for Improving Your Conversations

- Be the first to say hello.

- Introduce yourself to others.

- Display your sense of humor.

- Be receptive to new ideas.

- Make an extra effort to remember people's names.

- Ask a person's name if you have forgotten it.

- Show curiosity and interest in others.

- Be a good listener. The best conversationalists often talk the least and listen the most. (See section on Friendship Listening for tips on being a good listener.)

How to Talk to People with Whom You Have Nothing in Common

The key is to find as much common ground as possible. Try to appear more interested than interesting. Keep talking. Ask questions – you might learn something. Phrases such as "That's interesting: I'm not familiar with it," or "Explain that to me," help evoke more information.

Negative Party Talk

There is a negative person at every party. Negative people criticize the food, someone's outfit or the other guests. These people are usually so insecure about socializing that they resort to negative small talk in an effort to encourage further communication. This is not the way to show your wit and will often backfire.

Subjects to Avoid

- Your health

- Cost of things

- Mean gossip

- Off-color jokes

- Controversial issues (religion/politics)

Ending a Conversation

What do you do after a conversational subject has been exhausted? Don't wait until you or your partner feels the tension and becomes uncomfortable, nervous or visibly bored. Abruptly walking away or disappearing is also not a positive end to a conversation. The best time to end a conversation is when you have both expressed yourselves and when the time seems appropriate to part ways. Ending a conversation in a warm and personable manner will leave both of you feeling good about the encounter.

It is best not to try to escape by saying, "Excuse me, I need to go to the restroom," or "I need to refresh my drink," unless you are truly going to the restroom or refreshment area. Chances are you'll be caught if you don't go where you've said you are going. If you offer to get your conversational partner a drink while you're away, and the partner agrees to your offer, you'll have to return. A polite way to end the conversation is to sum up the conversation you've had (this acknowledges your conversational partner and shows that you have been listening), shake hands, and move on. Example, "Jill, I have enjoyed hearing about your backpacking trip to Yellowstone. Thanks for sharing your adventures with me. Take care and I hope to see your photographs soon."

THANK YOU NOTES

People who do nice things for you appreciate knowing that you like what they have done for you. Saying "thank you" is one way to let them know that you are grateful, and in our modern times of electronic communication, emails and faxes are additional ways to send an instant message of appreciation. However, the personal touch of a handwritten note has yet to be replaced. The Crane stationery ad is true, "To our knowledge no one has ever cherished a fax."

A well-written thank you note mentions:

1. The gift received or deed done for you.

2. How you used or will use the item you were given or significance of the deed done for you.

3. How much you appreciate the gift or what was done for you.

Writing a thank you note does not need to take a lot of time, but its impact can be great. The sooner you write the note, the less you'll need to write. The important thing to do is to write. People will appreciate your written thanks whether you write the note in pencil, on notebook paper, or on fine vellum. However, there are special types of paper from which you can choose and even certain types of writing instruments to use when your budget can bear a little extra expense. (See Correspondence and the Power of the Written Word.)

General Good Manners for Writing a Thank You Note

Thank people for having you as a guest for a special meal, party, overnight visit, gift, or for anything they have done especially nice for you such as help you with a difficult project.

Write and send your written note within a week after someone has done something special for you.

- Write your note on clean, nice paper.

- Use your best penmanship. Be neat.

- Use good grammar and look up the correct spelling of any words you do not know how to spell.

- Write your note as though you were talking to the person.

- Specifically tell the person you are thanking why you like the gift or appreciate what was done for you.

- Include a personal note about you and your family.

- Try to avoid beginning your thank-you note with "Thank you for..." For example, start your note by saying something like, "It was so much fun to be at your house Friday evening." Or "I appreciate you remembering me on my graduation."

Example of a generic letter that is not gracious

I really appreciated your gift. Thank you for thinking of me.

is not nearly as effective as

You remembered I collect teddy bears! How thoughtful of you to bring me a handmade collectible from your trip to California!

Write promptly, but remember it's never too late to send a note.

Example of a note to grandmother thanking her for a gift

Dear Grandmother,

The new easel is great! Now I can work on paintings without bending over the kitchen table! You are terrific for remembering me with the perfect gift.

Love,
Allison

Example of a note to someone who helped you

Dear Mrs. McComas,

I really appreciate your help in preparing me for the International Student Exchange program in Spain. I just got a letter saying that I have been accepted for a placement in Madrid. I can hardly wait! The time you spent with me helped me to prepare for the conversational part of my interview. Thanks so much!

Sincerely,
Brittany

Example of a note congratulating a friend

Dear Kyle,

I read the article about your victory in the essay contest. You must be so excited. I'm happy for you!

Your friend,
Allen

Example of a note of thanks for a party

Dear Margaret Ann,

  Your pool party was such fun! I enjoyed meeting your cousin and playing all of those games. Thanks again for inviting me.

As ever,

Alston

Writing Instruments

Formal thank you notes are written with ink pens. Black ink is traditional.

A Sample Thank You Letter

Dear Aunt Carol,

The paint ball equipment is awesome. The mask, hopper, elbo, co2 tank, and round of paint are just what I wanted. My friends and I are going out in the woods this weekend where we won't make a mess when we play paintball. I can't wait.

How do you, Uncle Pat, and my cousins Ginny, Katie and John like living in Japan? I bet it is interesting learning about the Japanese customs and traditions. We are thrilled that Uncle Pat was assigned there. He'll provide excellent leadership as Captain.

Our family is fine. Hanna is dancing almost every day, Dad stays busy at the hospital, and Mom still finds new flowers to plant and weeds to pull in the garden.

We hope to see you and the rest of the family during Thanksgiving.

Thanks again for a great present.

Love,
Chris

FORMS OF ADDRESS

When formally addressing a person in writing, use an honorific such as Mr., Mrs., Miss or Ms. in the salutation. The salutation in a friendly letter is followed by a comma.

Examples

Dear Mr. Williams,   Dear Mrs. Parker,
Dear Miss Covington,   Dear Ms. Wetherill,

Likewise, always include the honorific when addressing the envelope. A comma is not used. Write out the full name of a person when formally addressing an envelope.

Example

Mr. Thomas Abel Williams

When corresponding with a relative or close friend, it is correct to use their common given name in the salutation followed by a comma. However, do remember to use the honorific on the envelope.

Examples

Salutation:

Dear Aunt Barbara,   Dear Mrs. McMurry,
Dear Brenda,

Envelope:

Mrs. Henry Wesley Hight
Mrs. John Eugene McMurry   Miss Brenda Wright

When formally addressing an envelope to a young man aged 12 and under, use the honorific "Master." Use "Mr." after the age of 13.

Example

Master John Worthington Hand Stephenson, II (until the age of 13)
Mr. John Worthington Hand Stephenson, II (after the age of 13)

When addressing an envelope to a young girl or woman, use the honorific "Miss" until she is married or enters the business arena.

Example

Miss Allison Louise McMurry
Ms. Allison Louise McMurry
(when she enters the business arena)

When addressing an envelope to a divorced woman, the honorific "Mrs." is still appropriate, but use her first name instead of her former husband's name.

Example

Mrs. Brenda Mitwol

In the business arena, women are addressed by "Ms." and by first name regardless of marital status.

Example

Ms. Brenda Mitwol

When signing a greeting card, or listing your family by name, always list the mother's name first, then the father's, then list the children by age, from oldest to youngest.

Example

Jane, Gene, Winifred, and Allison McMurry
   Or
Jane and Gene McMurry
Winifred and Allison

"Simple speech is the best and truest eloquence."

Martin Luther, 1483-1546

SOCIAL CORRESPONDENCE STYLE

The Date and Address

Write the date on the first page at the top right of your social correspondence or on the last page below the signature and at the left margin. Social correspondence that is very formal requires nothing more than the day. For example, "Friday." You may abbreviate the month, as "Feb. 11th," in informal notes to friends, but in general save abbreviations for business correspondence.

It is optional to add your address to unmarked social correspondence paper. When you choose to include your address, write it on two lines at the end of your letter, below your signature and at the left margin. This placement avoids a business letter appearance.

Greetings and Closings for Social Letters Beginning with Dear

A greeting known as a salutation is always used to begin a social letter. Traditional social correspondence begins with "Dear," followed by a comma. The closing for a letter beginning with "Dear," should reflect the closeness to the person you are writing.

For people who are not your friends, acquaintances, a member of the opposite sex whom you know and simply like, or for someone you see socially on occasion, "As ever," is a good closing choice. Sometimes a friendly closing sentence followed by your name is the best solution. For example, "Your party was tops!" "Again, thanks for including us in your terrific party."

For people you know or deal with regularly, the phrase "With kindest regards," is a good closing. "Yours," is personal without being intrusive.

For all acquaintances, "Sincerely," "Sincerely yours," or "Yours truly," are good choices. Some people choose to use the word "Cordially," which I find friendly but somewhat formal.

For a very close relative who is older and someone seldom seen, popular closings are "Devotedly," "With love," and "Affectionately." A combination of the two closings "With love," and "Affectionately," may be used in which case they are placed on two separate lines."
For very close family and friends, you may choose to close with "Love," followed by a comma.

*Note: The salutation of traditional social correspondence to a family addresses only the female head of household. For example, a letter of thanks written to your aunt, uncle, and cousins begins with only "Dear 'Aunt Barbara.'" The body of the letter mentions the rest of the family you wish to thank. Likewise, the envelope bearing a social letter to a family is traditionally addressed to the female head of household using her correct social name. The envelope to "Aunt Barbara" is addressed to her using her correct social name, either informally, "Mrs. Henry Hight" or more formally, "Mrs. Henry Wesley Hight, Jr." However, it is not correct to address the letter to her using

the nickname of the uncle, for example, "Chip," as in "Mrs. Chip Hight." To address the envelope to "Aunt Barbara" or to "Mrs. Hight" is also incorrect.

Greetings and Closings for Social Letters Beginning with Dear Sirs or Gentlemen

The phrases "Dear Sirs:" and "Gentlemen:" are followed by a colon and are reserved for correspondence to people you do not know. However, always try to find out the name of the person who needs to read your correspondence. This personal effort on your part will be appreciated. Use the closing "Sincerely," or "Yours truly," for people you do not know.

Greetings and Closings to Avoid

Avoid the greetings "Dear Friend," and "To whom it may concern:" Find out the names of people you wish to address in writing. They will appreciate it and your letter is more likely to be favorably received.

Avoid the old-fashioned closing "Faithfully," and the distant sounding, "Best wishes." Avoid closing with a cliché such as "Thanking you in advance," which is presumptuous. Choose instead graceful closing phrases such as "I will appreciate..." or "I will be grateful..."

The Closing Line

Social correspondence often includes a final short phrase or sentence before the closing, such as "Gene sends his love," or "With love to Cindy." "The most formal closing line is "Please remember me to... 'your family,' '...your sister.'" The traditional closing after a closing line is "Sincerely," or "Devotedly." For business letters and not for social correspondence, use the closing line "With kindest regards," or "With regards to..." instead of the less desirable, "Give my regards to..."

Social Signatures for Women

The Signature of a Single Woman
A woman signs her name to all of her social correspondence. She may sign only her first name, "Allison," to informal correspondence to those she greets in the letter's salutation with a first name only or with her first and last names, "Allison McMurry," if the recipient of her letter may confuse her with someone else with the same first name. When the writer greets a person in the salutation with a surname (last name), the woman should sign the letter with her first and last names. The woman's full name, "Allison Louise McMurry," is the correct signature for formal social letters written by a woman. Honorifics such as" "Miss" "Mrs." "Ms." and "Dr." are not included with the signature.

It is correct to assume that a woman who does not indicate on her correspondence paper that she is married is single. However, a single woman who writes social letters to strangers on paper not printed with her full social name including her title may wish to let the recipient of the letter know the correct way to address any return correspondence in one of the following ways.

First, if she chooses, she may precede the signature of her name with the word "Miss" in parentheses, i.e., (Miss). For example,

Yours truly,

(Miss) Allison Louise McMurry

A second choice for the single woman is to write her name including the title below her signature, at the left-hand margin. This is the only correct placement if her address must also be included. For example,

Yours truly,

Allison Louise McMurry

Miss Allison Louise McMurry
708 Gimghoul Road
Chapel Hill, North Carolina 27514

A third choice that is less traditional for a single woman to use when giving her name without the address is to write it immediately under the signature in parentheses. For example,

Yours truly,

Allison McMurry
(Miss Allison Louise McMurry)

The Signature of a Married Woman

A married woman whose personal writing paper is not printed with her full social name including her title may wish to let the recipient of her letter know the correct way to address any return correspondence in one of the following ways.

The most correct form for a married woman is to write her married name below her signature, at the left-hand margin. This is the only correct placement if her address must also be included. For example,

Yours truly,

Jane H. McMurry

Mrs. John Eugene McMurry
2114 South Live Oak Parkway
Wilmington, North Carolina 28403

A second but less traditional choice for a woman to use if only the name is given without the address is to write it immediately under her signature in parentheses. For example,

Yours truly,

Jane H. McMurry
(Mrs. John Eugene McMurry)

Note: Placing (Mrs.) before the signature is not an option for a married woman as her correct social name includes the name of her husband. The neutral term "Ms." is not used as it does not indicate marital status. The honorific "Ms." is correctly used in business correspondence. However, a person returning social correspondence to a woman whose marital status is unknown should use the honorific "Ms." to address the woman.

Social Signatures for Men

A man signs his name to all of his social letters. The man signs his full name to formal social correspondence, for example, "John Eugene McMurry." He may sign only his first name, "John," to informal social correspondence to those he greets in the letter's salutation with a first name only or with his first and last names, "John McMurry," if the recipient of his letter may confuse him with someone else with the same first name. The man also signs his first and last names to correspondence when his salutation greets a person using a surname (last name).

A man who uses his middle name and not his first name often writes his first initial before his middle and last names. For example, "J. Eugene McMurry." The signature "J. E. McMurry" is not traditional and is not used unless people know the man by his initials or when the man has a first name that might be either masculine or feminine such as Jean or Leslie. In that event his signature "J. E. McMurry" or "J. Henry McMurry" or even "J. McMurry" if he has no middle name indicates gender to the reader so that he may be correctly addressed in future correspondence. In any event the man does not use the prefix "Mr." with or without parentheses to indicate gender before or below his signature nor does a man use any honorific such as "Mr." and "Dr." with his signature.

Envelopes

Start the address in the middle of the envelope. Write the name of the person the letter is to on the first line. Be sure to include the person's correct honorific. On the second line, write the street address; and on the third line, write the city, state (which should be spelled out in formal social correspondence) and zip code. The city and state are separated with a comma.

Example Showing the Correct Way to Address an Envelope

Mrs. Henry Wesley Hight
150 Country Club Drive
Henderson, North Carolina 27536

The sender's return address is correctly placed on the center of the back flap of an envelope containing a social note. However, The US Postal Service prefers the return address be placed on the front of the envelope on the upper left-hand corner, but does not require it. The return address for social correspondence traditionally does not include the sender's name.

Example Showing the Correct Way to Place a Return Address on the Back of an Envelope

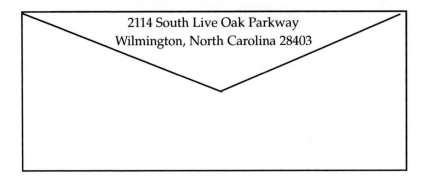

2114 South Live Oak Parkway
Wilmington, North Carolina 28403

Example Showing the Correct Way to Place a Return Address on the Front of an Envelope

2114 South Live Oak Parkway
Wilmington, North Carolina 28403

How to Put Letters and Notes in Envelopes

Place letters and notes in envelopes in a way that makes it easy for the person receiving the letter to get to its contents easily.

A Single or Double Sheet of Letter Paper

The opening page of a single or double sheet of letter paper is placed on top of multiple sheets in the correct order so that the opening page is inside the fold when the sheets are folded once across the center. The sheets are inserted fold first into the envelope. The top half of the opening page should face the back of the envelope.

A Long Single Sheet of Letter Paper

The long single sheet of letter paper is folded in three. The bottom third of the paper is first folded up over the center third of the paper. The slightly shorter top third is folded down over the bottom and middle third of the sheet. The letter paper is inserted lower fold first in the envelope. The top third of the paper should be against the back of the envelope. Place multiple single or double sheets of letter paper on top of each other in the correct order and fold them all together before putting them in the envelope.

A Double Sheet of Note Paper

It is not necessary to refold a double sheet of notepaper before placing it in its envelope which fits it exactly. The first page of the notepaper should always face the back of the envelope. If you write across the width of the paper, with the fold down the left side of the first page, the note should be inserted fold first. If you write across the length of the paper with the fold at the top, the note should be inserted fold last.

A Card With its Own Envelope

A card with its own envelope should be put in its envelope with the front of the card facing the back of the envelope.

"One kind word can warm three winter months."

Japanese Saying

SOCIAL WRITING PAPER

The hand-written note is a powerful tool in today's technological world. Receiving a hand-addressed letter on high-quality stationery is much more gratifying than a curled, faded, word-processed note that arrived via facsimile. A vast array of social stationery is available today ranging from formal to casual in style. Following is a list of some of the types of stationery you may want to have as you begin to correspond with family and friends. Keep a supply of your favorites on hand – it takes only a few minutes to write a quick note and its impact can be great and long lasting.

Calling Cards

The custom of the calling card is believed to have originated in China. Originally, a card engraved with a visitor's name was left in the door or with the servant when visiting a home and finding the owner absent. In the United States, this custom is only practiced in the military. Today we use calling cards as enclosure or gift cards. The cards may be formal and engraved with a single full name or the names of a married couple, or they may be more colorful and casual, bearing only one name. Calling cards are for use by men, women, and children.

Informal Folded Cards for Women

Informal folded cards are often incorrectly referred to as informals. They are small note cards folded across the top. These cards are typically used by women or married couples, but not by single men. They may be engraved or printed with the woman's name, name of a married couple, or the woman's complete married name. Informal folded cards are used for issuing or responding to invitations, sending brief notes, thank-you notes, or as gift enclosures. They are either white or ecru and printed with black ink. Writing begins on the inside, below the note's fold. Keep your message brief and do not write on the back of the card. Place the informal folded card into its envelope bottom edges first with the print facing the envelope flap so that the name will be seen first when the card is removed from its envelope.

Notes for Women

Notes are identical to the informal folded cards but are printed with the woman's monogram or her name written in full. Notes are used for the same purposes as informal folded cards and can be used for thank you notes.

Correspondence Cards for Men and Women

Correspondence cards are heavy weight cards marked with your name or monogram. They are available in plain ecru or white as well as bordered, and in a variety of colors. They range in style from very formal to casual and are used for brief notes, thank-you notes, holiday greetings and birthday wishes. Writing should be on the front side only. Place the correspondence card into its envelope bottom edge first with the writing facing the envelope flap so it will be most easily seen when the card is removed from its envelope. Men use correspondence cards instead of notes.

Half-Sheets for Men and Women

The half sheet is stationery paper that folds in half to fit in its envelope. Half sheets may be printed or engraved with a monogram, name and/or address. They are used for letters and thank you notes. Avoid writing on the back of the sheet and use a plain second sheet if you need room for a longer message.

Women's Formal Letter Sheets

Folded letter sheets are the most formal of social stationery. Formal letter sheets have a folded edge down the left side and are folded again in half from top to bottom to fit an envelope half its size. Formal letter sheets are ecru or white and can be printed with a name or monogram. These can be used for a variety of purposes including letters, thank you notes and issuing invitations. Plain unmarked formal letter sheets are the most correct stationery for a woman to use for issuing a wedding invitation or a letter of sympathy. Use black ink and begin writing on page one, then page three, and then page two if necessary. Write on the back of the sheet (page four) if necessary.

Men's Formal Social Writing Paper

Men use single sheets of good heavy quality paper that fits into a rectangular envelope when the sheet is folded once across the center. Black ink is used and writing does not continue onto the back of the sheet.

"Tis best wherever we are, to follow still the customs of the country."

Sophocles, 496?-406 B.C.

RESPONDING TO INVITATIONS

Invitations can range in formality from an engraved invitation for a wedding or black-tie event to an informal invitation or telephone call. All invitations require a response and the form of the invitation dictates the type of response required. Whenever you receive an invitation of any kind, decide as quickly as possible if you will attend and respond appropriately.

Lack of a response is high on the list of poor behavior never to be forgotten. The organizers of the event need to know how many people to expect in order to plan adequately for food, dancing, party favors, etc.

Respond in the manner in which the invitation is extended. If you receive a telephone call from someone inviting you to lunch, responding by telephone is appropriate. If you receive an e-mail from someone inviting you to dinner, responding by e-mail is appropriate. If you receive a formal written invitation that asks you to respond and provides a telephone number, again, respond via the telephone. The important thing is to respond.

*Note, invitations have not always asked for a response. Traditionally, an invitation issued by a well-mannered person expected a response from well-mannered people. In fact, to ask for a response was considered insulting on the part of the host as it implied that the person being issued the invitation did not know to reply to the invitation! The phrases "R.s.v.p." and "Regrets only" were finally added by frustrated hosts who needed a head count in order to correctly plan for a party. Always promptly respond to invitations.

How to Respond using a Reply Card

To respond using a provided reply card, simply fill in the information requested. Do not fill in any more than one in the space designated if the invitation was addressed to you alone. If the invitation was addressed to you and a spouse or partner, again do not include your visiting houseguests, your mother or your children.

How to Respond to a Formal Invitation

A formal invitation is extended in the third person and will usually have the words Rèpondez s'il vous plait or R. s. v. p. in the lower left-hand corner. This is French for "Respond if you please." This is intended as a command, not a suggestion. You should use a formal, folded letter sheet and write your response in the third person, using the following formula:

Example of a Handwritten Acceptance

Miss Hanna Catherine McMurry
accepts with pleasure
the kind invitation of
Mr. and Mrs. Geoffery Stuart Bitler
for Saturday, the fifth of July
from seven until nine in the evening

Example of a Handwritten Regret

Master Christopher Warren McMurry
regrets that he is unable to accept
the very kind invitation of
Mr. and Mrs. John Burke Haywood
for Saturday, the seventeenth of September

Today, many formal invitations include response cards that are simply filled in and mailed in the envelope provided. In any case, failure to respond is a grave social faux pas.

An Informal Response

A hand-written note accepting or declining an informal invitation is always acceptable, but it is obligatory when the informal written invitation has the words "R.s.v.p." or "Regrets only" written on the bottom left of the invitation. Respond by sending a simple hand-written note. For example,

Dear Catherine,

Gene and I will be delighted to join you for dinner Sunday, the fifteenth of December.

Regards,
Jane

Informal written invitations often have the words "R.s.v.p." or "Regrets only" along with a telephone number. The correct way to respond as mentioned earlier is by telephoning your intent.

As technology evolves so does etiquette. I am beginning to see invitations that include an e-mail address beside the "R.s.v.p." and "Regrets only" portion of the invitation. It is good manners to respond to the invitation in the manner your host's invitation requests. When a telephone or e-mail address is included beside "R.s.v.p." respond using the appropriate technology. "Regrets only" requires that you respond only if you do not plan to attend. However you respond, *respond*, and respond promptly.

DEVELOPING AND MAINTAINING FRIENDSHIPS

Developing and maintaining friendships is important to most people. Some people seem to easily make and keep friends, others find it difficult and they constantly are lonely. To develop a real friendship takes work and time, but the rewards make the effort worth it. Real friendship means sharing the good and the bad. It means caring about someone other than yourself and helping others whenever possible.

Who Will Be Your Friends

The easiest people to develop a relationship with are people who share similar interests, values and goals as you. Join activity groups that interest you - you're sure to meet people who like the same things that you do! If you like art, take an art class and meet people who like to draw and paint. If you like soccer, join a soccer league. Our world is teeming with people who like art, music, sports and the great outdoors. Put yourself in places where people who share your interests, values and goals are and you'll find people you'll enjoy having as friends.

Valued Friendship Qualities

A real friend is one of the most valuable treasures you can have. A real friend is also one of the best things you can be. Be a friend, and you'll have friends. Examine the following list of friendship qualities, but instead of comparing your friends to it, take the list and compare yourself to it.

- Trustworthiness
- Loyalty
- Kindness
- Supportiveness
- Honesty
- Humility
- Tactfulness

- Openness
- Sincerity
- Patience
- Punctuality
- Respectfulness
- Willingness to Share
- Sense of Humor

Friendship Building Blocks

- *Share Yourself*
  Think about what you can give to a friend and not what you can get out of a friendship. Avoid keeping track of who has given what in a friendship. Practice giving to your friends regardless of what they give or do for you.

- *Listen to Your Friends*
  Focus on what the other person is saying. People like people who listen when they need to talk. People dislike people who always talk about themselves and their problems.

- *Commit Yourself to Your Friends*
  Develop a sense of friendship by sharing experiences. Volunteer to participate in activities like community service projects or musicals and show that you are reliable and dependable once you commit yourself.

- *Accept Differences in Friends*
  Friends do not always think the same way. Agree to disagree if you have a discussion with a friend and the friend disagrees with you. Avoid arguing that results in anger. Stop a discussion that becomes heated because the battle to win an argument often ruins a friendship.

- *Support Your Friend's Goals and Achievements*
  Real friends encourage each other to be the best they can be and are happy when friends achieve goals.

- *Accept the Humanness of Your Friend*
  No one is perfect. When your friend makes a mistake realize that (s)he is human and that everyone makes mistakes sometimes. A real friend will tactfully point out a problem but not dwell on it. Flaws are often difficult to detect in oneself – remember this if a friend points out something you're doing wrong!

- *Friends Forgive*
  Friends do make mistakes and sometimes they realize it without having it pointed out. Forgive your friend when (s)he apologizes and asks for forgiveness. Never let hurt turn into a grudge. Harboring a grudge is a sure way to destroy any friendship.

- *Friends are Trustworthy*
  Friends keep each other's secrets. Breaking a confidence is sometimes okay when telling will help the friend. This exception is for circumstances like friends who tell you about a serious problem like

drugs, alcohol, stealing, deep depression or an eating disorder. Encourage your friend to talk to a trusted adult about the problem. Tell the friend that you feel that as a friend you must go for help for his/her own safety if he refuses to seek help. The friend may become angry with you, but true friendships are worth the risk. The friendship may be lost, but a friend's life may be saved.

- *Friends Allow Each Other Freedom*
  Real friends allow each other time with other people. Controlling and dominating a friendship by trying to be with the friend all the time smothers a good relationship. True friends endure separations.

- *Friends are Dependable*
  Friends can count on each other. Keep your promises.

Question: What is a Good Friend?
Answer: A Person Who
... consistently treats others with kindness
... sticks up for us when no one else will
... does not make fun of us or those we love
... includes everyone in activities - even if a person is not very good
... shares
... compliments others when a job is done well
... admits when he or she is wrong and says, "I'm sorry"
... has a good sense of humor but not at the expense of others

Question: Who is not a Good Friend?
Answer: A Person Who

... whispers secrets and leaves others out

... is a bully and picks on people

... gossips

... cheats

... is a poor sport

... is conceited and brags

... thinks he is superior to others

... points out our weaknesses

Remember

Be a friend and you'll have friends. After all, good friends are always in demand.

Eleanor Roosevelt had the following to say about friendship.

Many people will walk in and out of your life,
But only true friends will
Leave footprints in your heart.

To handle yourself, use your head;
To handle others, use your heart.
Anger is only one letter short of danger.
Great minds discuss ideas;
Average minds discuss events;
Small minds discuss people.
He who loses money, loses much;
He who loses a friend, loses much more;
He who loses faith, loses all.
Beautiful young people are accidents of nature,
But beautiful old people are works of art.

FRIENDSHIP LISTENING

People listen for lots of reasons. Listening for information is practiced at school. Listening for enjoyment is practiced at concerts and at movies. Friendship listening is the special type of listening we do with a friend or with anyone with whom we hope to have a peaceful relationship.

A good listener practices good listening skills just as an athlete or dancer practices to perfect certain physical skills.

Friendship listening is not automatic for we are not born knowing how to understand what we hear anymore than we are born knowing how to dance or play soccer. However, skills necessary for developing and maintaining friendships can be learned just as dancing and sporting skills can be learned. Once we learn the steps, it is important to practice.

Friendship listening is listening with complete attention to your friend and then repeating back in your own words what the friend said. This way your friend knows that you have listened and understood.

Practice These Friendship Listening Steps

Step One: **Look at your friend while [s]he is talking.** Maintain eye contact and a pleasant expression. Remember not to fidget or laugh at your friend.

Step Two: **Think about the meaning of what your friend is telling you and try to understand what your friend is feeling from his/her point of view.**

Many people are so busy formulating their response that they do not listen to the ideas and thoughts of their conversation partner.

Step Three: **Don't interrupt or finish someone's sentence.** Some people take longer than others to formulate a sentence or choose the right word. A thoughtful, well-mannered person waits for the other person to finish a sentence before jumping in with his own interpretation.

Step Four: **Don't look away, over someone's shoulder or at your watch.** You'll appear disinterested or distracted.

Step Five: **Repeat back to your friend what [s]he has told you.** Do this in your own words. This important step lets your friend know that his/her feelings have been heard. If you don't understand what your friend has told you, it is appropriate to ask questions related to what [s]he has told you.

Step Six: **Avoid judging, criticizing or telling your friend what to do about a problem.** Do encourage your friend to find a solution to his/her problem.

EXPRESSING YOUR PROBLEMS

The Positive "I" vs. The Negative "You"

Problems. Everyday, somebody has a problem with a teacher, a parent, a friend or an acquaintance. Solving problems with others requires talking – not fighting – and sometimes talking with others about the problem can cause even more problems! The people who have the fewest problems are usually those who have problem solving skills.

All people with problems can choose to talk about their feelings in one of two ways. One way of talking will create a positive climate in which problems can be worked out, the other way of talking will create a negative climate where problems may become worse.

Talk that evaluates or criticizes establishes a negative atmosphere because the speaker sounds as if he is blaming or finding fault with the listener. This negative talk usually begins with the word "you." The listener immediately is put on the defensive and builds an imaginary wall to protect himself. For example, a listener who hears, "You are a jerk. Your loud music is dumb," immediately turns off and wants to protect himself by verbally or physically attacking the speaker or by fleeing the situation.

Talk that describes the way the speaker feels creates a positive climate for solving conflicts. The speaker who positively approaches problem solving usually begins her/his statements with the word "I." This speaker accepts responsibility for his feelings. The atmosphere the speaker creates is not threatening to the listener so discussion of the problem can take place and conflict resolution has a chance. For example, the listener who hears, "I am anxious about the math test tomorrow. I have a hard time studying when I hear loud music," is more likely to turn down the music than if being told he is a jerk and likes dumb music.

Using "I" language does not necessarily mean that your problems will be solved or that you will get what you want. However, "I" language will open the door to discussion instead of slamming the door. Create the opportunity for better understanding by practicing "I" language.

Examples of 'I' vs. 'You' Language

The following pairs of sentences are examples of the positive and negative feelings that can be created by simply using positive "I Language" or negative "You Language."

- *You* give us too much work and never completely explain the assignments.
  vs/
- *I* feel frustrated when I stay up late at night to do my homework and discover the next day that my effort was incorrect.

- *You* are mean and unfair not to let me hang-out at the mall with my friends.
  vs.
- *I* feel left out when my friends go to the mall and I have to stay at home.

- *You* are a liar. You told me you would not tell anyone my secret.
  vs.
- *I* am hurt and embarrassed that everybody knows my secret.

- *You* never play with me.
  vs.
- *I* feel sad when I have to be alone.

- *You* make me angry when you mess up my room.
  vs.
- *I* feel frustrated when I find the room I organized, messed up.

- *You* make me mad when you wear my new clothes.
  vs.
- *I* feel taken advantage of when my new clothes are worn without my permission.

- *You* are terrible to pick me up late from school.
  vs.
- *I* worried that something had happened to you when you didn't pick me up on time.

- *You* are a selfish pig.
  vs.
- *I* am angry when all the cake has been eaten and I didn't get a single piece.

EVERYONE WINS WITH WIN-WIN

Conflict is unavoidable. When conflict occurs there are three possible outcomes:

- *YOU* can win.
- The *OTHER PERSON* can win.
- You can *BOTH* win.

HOW TO WIN-WIN

1. Each side needs to take time to cool off before reacting to problems in a way that later might be regretted. Each side expresses anger in a way that will not cause problems with others - for example, an angry person may hit tennis balls against a backboard or go for a jog instead of lashing out at another person.

2. Each side states feelings and the problem as it sees it by using "I language." Each side is careful to avoid blaming, name-calling and interrupting.

3. Each side states the problem as the other side sees it. (This step shows that each side is listening to the other.)

4. Each side says how it is responsible for the problem. ("I language" is used.)

5. Both sides brainstorm solutions and choose a solution that is agreeable to both sides. This solution is a win-win solution.

6. Each side affirms the other – that is each side notices and tells the other what is positive or special about the other.

Social skills like win-win can be learned just as social dancing can be learned. Both take practice. *The Dance Steps of Life*™ are worth the effort.

MAGIC WORDS

The words we choose to use can help us get what we want and help people have a good feeling when they are around us. Use the following words often and you'll see doors open to you as if by magic!

Thank-you

Please

May I?

Excuse me

Pardon me

I'm sorry

After you

You first

Your choice

You choose

Great job

Good going

I need your help

You're a big help

You're great, smart, fun

Great idea

Good thinking

Congratulations

"A gossip is one who talks to you about others; a bore is one who talks to you about himself; and a brilliant conversationalist is one who talks to you about yourself."

Lisa Kirk, 1954
New York Journal American

GIVING AND RECEIVING COMPLIMENTS

Giving Compliments

Giving compliments to others is a friendly way to begin a conversation and to promote goodwill. Compliments make others feel good. Give them whenever you honestly can. The one rule is that the compliment must be sincere. You can compliment others directly, indirectly, privately and in front of others.

The following tips will make you an expert in complimenting others.

- Compliment with sincerity and be careful not to gush. If you like a person's sweater, simply tell them with a phrase like, "What a beautiful sweater." Avoid going on and on about the color, style, weave etc. which could make boring conversation. Adding a comment such as, "That sweater is better looking than the red one you wore yesterday" detracts from the compliment.

- Indirect compliments are compliments that let the other person know that you admire or value something about him/her without directly saying so. An opportunity to give indirect compliments often arises when you want assistance. For example, "This sweater is bulkier than ones I usually wear. You know so much about fashion, I'd really appreciate your opinion." Secondhand compliments are also an indirect way of making others feel good. For example, "Spencer told me that your serve was awesome on the tennis courts yesterday."

- Giving compliments in the presence of others must be done with sensitivity to others who are present. Avoid giving a compliment to one person that might be interpreted as an insult to the others. For example, if you tell one person what a beautiful sweater (s)he is wearing, the others present and wearing sweaters may feel that you are implying that you don't like theirs.

Receiving Compliments

Compliments are like gifts and deserve no less. Always let the giver know that you appreciate the gift of a compliment. In the United States it is appropriate to say "Thank you," "I'm glad you like it," "What a nice thing to say," or "I appreciate that." Responding to a compliment by denying it with a remark such as "This faded sweater is an old hand-me-down that has a hole under the arm, etc." is rude and may make the compliment giver feel that you don't respect or value his opinion. Europeans receive compliments without words by giving a friendly smile. Asians acknowledge with a gracious bow. As you can see, the universal etiquette custom of receiving compliments is to return a compliment of goodwill with a gesture of gracious appreciation.

THE GOOD HOST

Friends and acquaintances will enjoy visits with you if you know how to be a good host. Four steps can make you a popular host and your home a favorite place for friends to visit.

Step One: **Extend an invitation to your guest.** Make clear the beginning and ending time of the invitation. Let your guest know if the invitation includes any special activity requiring special clothing.

Step Two: **Prepare for your guest.** Make the environment one in which positive interaction can take place. Place out of sight any special objects that you do not want others to touch. Prepare for overnight guests by putting clean sheets on the bed and placing clean linen in the bathroom. Plan and prepare refreshments for your guests.

Step Three: **Plan activities.** Have a few activities in mind and let your guest choose. Choose something in which two people can participate. It's not much fun watching one person playing computer games meant for one person. Avoid activities that prevent you and your guest from enjoying each other. TV and video games are for times when you are alone. (Exception, extended guest visits may welcome a conversation/interaction break).

Step Four: **Make the guest feel welcome.** A host's number-one priority is the comfort of his guest. Always greet your guest at the door. Smile and say "Thank-you for coming!" Take the person's coat, backpack or other belongings. Introduce a new friend to your family. Old friends should greet your family, too! Offer something to eat or drink. Even if you're not hungry or thirsty, your guest may be. The good host puts his guest's wishes before his own. Remember: The guest is always right, gets to choose the activities, and is served the first and biggest piece of pie! Your guest's honor is to win an argument and to select the games to play. The exception is if the guest chooses an activity that may be harmful to anyone or to personal property.

Step Five: **Never criticize your guest.**

Step Six: **Be loyal to your guest.** Never leave your guest alone for more than a few minutes unless your guest has come for an extended visit for several days and therefore may crave some private time. If someone calls for you, politely say, "I have company right now. May I call you back later?" Talking on the telephone when you have a guest is rude! Walk your guest to the door to say good-bye when your guest leaves. If you are young and your parents are driving your guest home, you should ride along too. Say "Thanks for coming! I had a great time with you."

THE GOOD GUEST

You will be a popular guest if you know the steps of a Good Guest.

Step One: **Arrive and depart on time.** If the host has not made clear the beginning and ending invitation time, ask. Greet your friend and immediately find adult hosts and say hello. Say hello to other family members, too.

Step Two: **Wear and/or pack appropriate clothing.** Ask your host if you need any special clothing or athletic equipment. Extended visits usually require extra clothing. Pack for the unexpected.

A raincoat, party dress, or coat and tie may be needed when you will be visiting for several days. If your friend doesn't offer to take your coat when you arrive, ask, "Where should I hang my coat?" Don't drape your coat over a chair or lay your backpack on the floor. If your shoes are wet or dirty, take them off and ask your friend where to put them.

Step Three: **Respect the rules of the house.** If breakfast is served at 7 am, be dressed and at the table at 7 sharp. Go to bed when your host signals. Your host should offer you something to eat or drink. If you're thirsty, you may ask for a drink of water. A perceptive host will say "Of course! Would you prefer some juice or a coke?" If the person gives you a glass of water when you really wanted to be offered something else, accept it graciously. Help clear your place and put any dishes you use into the dishwasher after a snack or meal.

Step Four: **Never criticize your host.** Eat what is offered and join in the planned activities. Your host may let you choose the activities. Ask what activities he/she prefers and let those suggestions guide you in your choice. Readily take turns.

Step Five: **Be loyal to your host.** Other guests or family members may attract your attention. Remember that a good guest does not divert attention from his host.

Step Six: **Be tidy.** Leave any area you spend time in as nice or nicer than you found it. Make your bed. Consider that others may need to use a shared bathroom. Hang up used towels. Flush. Place books or games back on the shelf. Turn off the lights. Close the doors. Do not interrupt others who are busy or enter rooms with closed doors. Offer to help in the kitchen when appropriate. Don't be nosy — don't wander into various rooms of the house or open drawers or closets. Don't read mail or notes that may be lying about. Don't comment on personal items that may be hanging on the refrigerator.

Step Seven: **Be a conversational pro.** Remember that the best conversationalists often talk the least and listen the most. Avoid tying up the telephone and making long distance calls charged to your host. Ask before using the telephone.

Step Eight: **Express thanks.** Thank your host for his hospitality before you leave. Hosts and hostesses appreciate a thank you note from guests who come for an extended visit. Host gifts such as a box of chocolate, flowers, or a best selling book are appropriate gifts of thanks for a special visit.

DRESS CODES

Jeans and tees?
Coats and dresses?
Do you know that clothes send messages?

The Scottish tartan names the clan, the shoe reflects the athlete's sport and the uniform (style and color) reflects occupation, rank or military service branch.

Once upon a time, kings banned non-royalty from wearing specific clothing styles and rich fabrics. Corduroy was literally the cloth of kings. In today's non-fairy tale times, modern mandates require certain attire in private clubs, private schools, businesses, and athletic competitions. To go against the unofficial laws of dress might not result in king-decreed death today, but it certainly could cause loss of privilege and opportunity. The socially smart investigate and learn the club rules.

Today's tribal togs reflect the group people belong to or to which they wish to belong, be it in Togo or in Texas. "Anything goes" absolutely never goes! People wear clothes that reflect their social attitudes and social choices. Students who fit in wear clothes acceptable to their friends. Well-informed travelers wear clothing acceptable to the nations they visit. For example, Arab countries require women in public to completely cover their bodies. A bikini in Saudi Arabia would be a big taboo!

The outcast is often the person who does not dress in clothing acceptable to the members of the group to which (s)he wishes to belong. In fact, the non-wearer sends the non-verbal message that (s)he rejects that group! Some creative clothing is acceptable as an expression of individuality, but generally, it takes great charm to successfully wear it, especially on a consistent basis.

The primary consideration when choosing clothes is that others will be looking at you more than you will be looking at yourself. Consider how people make each other feel when they look at each other. Good? Grossed out? Disgusted? Good manners mean making others feel at ease. To make others feel comfortable it is important for the person to first feel comfortable with her/himself. People usually feel more comfortable when they fit in and are a bit underdressed rather than overdressed. However, a greatly underdressed guest often appears insulting to his/her host, as it seems that the guest did not take polite interest in considering the type of invitation. Polite people take time to present themselves in a way that is pleasing to others. The best way to begin this polite presentation is with good grooming.

DRESS DETAILS FOR WOMEN

"Fine feathers do not always make fine birds."

Richard Wells, 1890
Manners, Customs, and Dress

General Tips

Simple, well-cut clothes are the best clothing choice because they will not go out of style. Undergarments that show prevent a polished look so be sure to inspect your clothing in the mirror. Choose clothes that flatter your shape and avoid clothes that cling to your figure. Wear stockings in harmony with your shoes.

Hats

Hats can be the glory of an outfit and better yet can save your skin from the sun's harmful rays. If you choose to wear a hat, pick one that flatters your face.

The etiquette for women concerning hats goes back to medieval times when women often wore jeweled wigs and elaborate hats. Removal of a hat could have jolted a fine wig's precarious position. Thus, a well-bred woman never removed her hat when inside or outside of buildings. The same holds true today, except thoughtfulness of others - our standard of courtesy today - requires that a woman remove her hat in situations where a hat might obstruct another's view.

Gloves

The custom of wearing gloves is very old. In Egyptian hieroglyphics, the glove symbolizes the hand. Gloves originally were worn for protection from cold weather and from the danger of battle. In the Middle Ages, women began to wear gloves for fashion.

Today women still wear gloves for protection and fashion. The custom of when to leave on gloves and when to remove them hinges on the past.

Knights removed their gauntlets to offer a bare and vulnerable hand as a sign of friendship and as an act of faith. Today if you are wearing gloves and you are introduced to someone who is not, remove your gloves to shake hands. Knights and members of the royal court removed their gloves when eating. Today as in the age of knights, remove gloves when eating.

Long gloves are still worn at very formal dances in America and in other parts of the world. Women do not need to remove gloves when shaking hands. Gloves are left on at dances, receptions and in receiving lines. The custom is to wear bracelets over and rings under gloves. Women remove gloves before eating, drinking, playing cards or applying makeup. Long, elbow length gloves should be removed as soon as a woman is seated at a dining table. Gloves are never placed on the table or the arms of chairs. Women wearing gloves with buttons at the wrist who do not wish to remove them when dancing or drinking, may remove just the hand part and roll that part of the glove inward towards the wrist and tuck it under.

Glove wearing customs vary throughout the world. For example, in the northern parts of Europe, but not in the southern, it is the custom to shake hands with gloves on, off, or rolled back and to drink and dance with gloves rolled back or off. However, a universal custom is to completely remove gloves when dining or when being wed.

Today, common sense prevails over chivalry. If it's cold outside, leave your gloves on to shake hands. Formal gloves worn for fashion, especially long kid gloves that do not have buttons and are difficult to remove may be left on when shaking hands both here and abroad.

Hand-bags

Choose handbags that are in proportion to your size and appropriate to your outfit.

Jewelry

Wear minimal jewelry for daytime events.

"A monkey in silk is still a monkey."

Spanish Saying

DRESS DETAILS FOR MEN

"I hold that gentleman to be the best dressed whose dress no one observes."

Anthony Trollope

General Tips

Men will find that choosing well-cut clothes that fit properly are the best clothing choice because they will not go out of style. Undergarments that show prevent a polished look so be sure to inspect your clothing in the mirror. Choose clothes that flatter your shape and avoid clothes that hug your body. Wear dark socks with dress shoes.

Belts

Dark belts are generally more practical and typically match the color of the leather shoes with which they are worn. Choose buckles that do not attract attention.

Pockets

Keep the top outside pocket of a jacket neat – avoid stuffing pens and handkerchiefs inside and poking out. The best place for a wallet, pens, and pencils is in the inside jacket pocket – not the back pocket of your trousers. It is handy to carry a handkerchief in your inside pocket.

You never know when you might need to wipe cuts or tears! And, my final advice concerning pockets is that you keep your hands out of them. A man with his hands thrust into his pockets appears insecure and is not readily able to shake hands with others.

Neck Ties

Croatian soldiers in the 18th century were the first to wear neckties. King Louis XIV liked the look, adapted it, wore it and called it a "cravat." The necktie-wearing trend begun by French royalty is still worn by well-dressed men. Today the English call it a cravat; Americans simply call it a tie.

Well-dressed men know how to tie bow and neckties correctly. Follow these simple diagrams and you'll quickly master techniques for tying a tie.

How to Tie a Bow Tie

- Start with one end about one and one-half inches below the other and bring the long end through the center.

- Form a loop with the short end and center it where the knot will be.

- Bring the long end over it.

- Form a loop with the long end and push it through the knot behind the front loop.

- Adjust the ends slowly so that they are about the same on either side of the knot.

How to Tie a Half Windsor Knot

- Place the tie around your neck with the wider end hanging on the right side of your chest about twelve inches below the narrow end which is hanging over the left side of your chest.

- Cross the wide end over the narrow end and pull it around and underneath the narrow end.

- Carry the wide end up through the loop and pass it around the front from left to right.

- Bring the wide end through the loop again and pass it through the knot in front.

- Tighten the knot slowly as you draw it up to the collar.

How to Tie a Four-in Hand Knot

- Place the tie around your neck with the wider end hanging on the right side of your chest about twelve inches below the narrow end which is hanging over the left side of your chest.

- Cross the wide end over the narrow end and pull it up through the loop.

- Hold the front of the knot loosely with the index finger and pull the wide end through the loop in front.

- Tighten the knot slowly while holding the narrow end and sliding the knot to the collar.

Hats

Sports hats are perhaps the most popular hats worn by men today. However, the etiquette for wearing hats in modern times harks back to the age of chivalry. Knights of the Middle Ages wore full armor in public. Knights raised helmet visors as a sign of mutual recognition. The knight removed his helmet entirely when in the company of friends. The complete removal of his helmet symbolized his belief that he was safe among friends and without need of his protecting helmet. One of the ways a well-mannered man shows respect for others is by remembering the following pointers.

- He removes his hat when being introduced or saying good-bye.

- He removes his hat while talking with a woman, an older man, or any person he wishes to show special respect.

- He raises his hat in recognition of a friend when passing and removes his hat completely in the presence of an assembly of friends.

- He removes his hat with his left hand leaving his right hand free to shake hands – or removes with right and transfers to the left hand.

- He tips his hat to an acquainted woman he meets on the street and removes it completely when speaking to her. He may replace his hat if he and the woman walk ahead together.

- He removes his hat inside all buildings.

- He removes his hat and stands for the national anthem.

- He removes his hat when he says the pledge of allegiance and when the American flag passes in a parade.

- He removes his hat in an apartment-house or hotel elevator.

- He removes his hat at solemn outdoor ceremonies, such as a burial.

* *A man does not remove his hat in Orthodox Jewish synagogues and some Conservative synagogues, stores, lobbies, corridors, and elevators of public buildings such as stations and post offices.*

Gloves

The custom of wearing gloves is very old. In Egyptian hieroglyphics, the glove symbolizes the hand. Gloves originally were worn for protection from cold weather and from the danger of battle. Today people still wear gloves for protection and fashion. The custom of when to leave on gloves and when to remove them hinges on the past.

Knights removed their gauntlets to offer a bare and vulnerable hand as a sign of friendship and as an act of faith. Today if you are wearing gloves and you are introduced to someone who is not, remove your gloves to shake hands. Knights removed their gloves when eating. Today as in the age of knights, men remove gloves when eating.

Men remove gloves when shaking hands with women. The man may leave his gloves on without apologizing if it is too awkward and time consuming to remove his gloves. Men remove gloves when inside buildings unless the gloves are part of a wedding ensemble or dress for a fancy ball.

Blazers, Sports Coats, Jackets

• Jackets look best that are long enough to cover the seat of trousers.

- The lower button on a two-button jacket should be at belt level.

- The middle button on a three-button jacket should be at belt level.

- Jacket sleeves should reach the base of the hands when the arms are held straight.

- Jacket collars should fit closely around the back of the neck.

- Shirt collars should show about half an inch above the jacket at the back of the neck.

- Shirt cuffs look best when they show about half an inch below the sleeve of the jacket when your arm is held down.

- The base of the trousers should rest on the top of the shoes and be slightly longer at the back of the shoe where they should drop to the top of the heel.

Vests

- Leave the lowest button unbuttoned.

Socks

- Wear socks long enough to avoid exposing the leg when sitting.

- Wear plain, dark socks.

Jewelry for Men

Men traditionally have worn little or no jewelry. Well-dressed men have chosen simple jewelry such as wristwatches and perhaps a signet ring. Today's modern man often opts to wear jewelry now acceptable that was once considered taboo for a man in certain groups. The choice is for today's man to make.

Trouble arises when deciphering dress codes such as

- Come as you are

- Don't bother to change

- Come for dinner (or some other outing)

- Casual

- Informal

- Semi-Formal

- Formal

Question: What's a well-mannered guest to do?

Answer: Read the section DECIPHERING DRESS CODES.

DECIPHERING DRESS CODES

The following definitions are suitable for both women and men:

Come As You Are

- Flatter your host and interpret the invitation to mean that it is expected you'll be wearing neat and clean clothes.

Don't Bother To Change

- Change into neat, clean, casual clothes

Come For Dinner Or Other Outing

- Ask the host what to wear. Asking demonstrates the guest's desire to wear appropriate apparel and shows that the invitation is appreciated. A considerate host will tell her guests what to expect if the guests are not accustomed to the host's style of entertaining.

Many invitations to parties will give information telling you what type of clothing to wear. The following guidelines will help you determine what to wear.

Casual For Women

- Casual shirt (blouse, polo, tee-shirt)
- Sweater
- Shorts, pants or jeans, casual skirt

- Socks or stockings in harmony with shoes
- Flat shoes (neutral color or in tone of clothing)

Casual For Men

- Casual shirt (polo, tee-shirt)
- Sweater
- Shorts or jeans

Informal For Women

- Daytime dress or skirt and blouse
- Daytime slacks and blouse (not jeans)
- Stockings that are in harmony with shoes
- Dressy or low-heeled shoes neutral in color in tone with clothing

Informal For Men

- Jacket
- Shirt (may be worn without a tie. Shirt collars stay inside the jacket)
- Slacks
- Dark socks (black, dark grey, dark blue)
- Dark shoes (black or brown)
- See section on Coats and Ties

Semi-Formal For Women

- Dressy dress or party dress
- Dressy slacks are also generally acceptable THOUGH IT IS IMPORTANT TO NOTE that some elegant American and European restaurants will not accept slacks on women!
- Dressy flat or heeled shoes neutral in color or in tone with clothing

Semi-Formal For Men

- Suit
- Necktie or bow tie
- Blue blazer with slacks or suit
- Dark socks without patterns (black preferred)
- See section on Coats and Ties

The term Formal attire includes Morning Dress, Evening Dress (commonly called Black Tie), and Full Evening Dress (commonly called White Tie).

Morning Dress For Women

Worn to weddings, garden parties, ceremonies before noon

- Elegant suit
- Dressy dress
- Hat (optional)
- Gloves

- Dressy flat or heeled shoes neutral in color or in tone of clothing

Morning Dress For Men

Worn at weddings by a groom and his groomsmen in a wedding occurring before noon. Also worn by men at very special occasions occurring before noon. (Example: The Royal Ascot Races in England)

- Black or grey morning coat
- Grey vest
- White shirt with stiff collar
- Silver tie with pearl tie pin
- Striped trousers
- Black top hat or grey top hat (the grey top hat is sometimes called a white hat)
- Grey gloves
- Black socks
- Black patent leather shoes or black leather shoes

Evening Dress/Black Tie For Women

- Elegant evening short dress *or*
- Elegant evening long dress *or*
- Elegant evening blouse and slacks *or*
- Elegant evening suit
- Stockings in harmony with choice of dress
- Elegant dressy flat or heeled shoes neutral in color or tone with clothing

Evening Dress/Black Tie For Men

Evening dress is referred to in conversation as "dinner jacket" or "black tie" (not tuxedo) and is worn to very formal dinners and dances. A groom and his groomsmen would wear Black Tie attire in a wedding occurring between one o'clock and five o'clock in the afternoon. The attire includes

- Tailless black jacket or very dark blue wool in a light weight, either double – or single-breasted, with a plain collar, peaked lapels faced with satin or grosgrain faille fabric. The single-breasted jacket may be cut with a shawl collar and is usually satin-faced. A variation is the white dinner jacket with shawl collar (faced with the same material) that is often worn with black slacks and cummerbund in summer.

- Black trousers which match the black jacket. (Trousers are not cuffed and have a single black braid or satin trim down the outside leg of the trousers.)

- Suspenders – not a belt.

- White shirt, often pleated.

- Black cummerbund or waistcoat (vest) with a single-breasted dinner jacket. The cummerbund or waistcoat is usually made of wool to match the jacket, or of black plain or figured silk.

- White shirt with a pleated front and fold collar. (Sometimes a plain white shirt with a well-fitting collar is worn, but not a button-down collar.)

- Bow tie of plain dull black silk, satin, or velvet, but not brocade.

- Black socks made of silk or nylon.

- Black shoes without toe caps. Shoes may be patent leather or fine, thin leather with a high polish.

Other colors and Patterns:

- Various colors and patterns are available for men to wear. I enjoy the happy mood men's clothing may make especially during the holidays. One man I know wears an heirloom Christmas waistcoat. Another wears an elegant needle-pointed cummerbund with a safari motif. However, be careful if you select a variation from traditional clothing. The man without great charm who wears variations often looks like an entertainer.

Optional:

- Overcoat of black, very dark blue, or Oxford grey smooth cloth (not tweed), with or without a velvet collar.

- Scarf. White silk is the most traditional. (Sometimes scarves are monogrammed in black, white, or grey.)

- Hat. The black Homburg is traditional.

- Gloves that are chamois or grey suede.

Formal Full Evening Dress or White Tie For Women

Worn on the most formal occasions beginning after six o'clock in the evening.

- Glamorous long dress

- Showy evening jewelry

- Long gloves (see gloves section)

- Socks or stockings in harmony with shoes

- Elegant dressy flat or heeled shoes neutral in color or tone with clothing

Formal Full Evening Dress or White Tie For Men

Worn on the most formal occasions beginning after six o'clock in the evening. Formal dress is often referred to as "white tie," or simply as "tails." It is considered mandatory to wear "White Tie" apparel when the invitation specifies "White Tie" or "Decorations," or if one is a member of a wedding party, or a father of the bride or groom at a very formal evening wedding, or the escort of a girl making her debut at a formal private dance or group ball. Formal full evening dress is very traditional, and never changes. The traditional clothing includes:

- Black tail coat or midnight blue wool with satin lapels. The tails should hang to a point just behind the knees.

- Dress trousers which match the coat. The trousers usually have two rows of black satin trim or braid down the outside of the trouser legs.

- White stiff-fronted shirt with separate wing collar. The traditional shirt is made of fine white linen or piqué. The shirt is made for one or two studs, and has starched cuffs.

- White bow tie, usually of white piqué.

- White piqué waistcoat (vest), with or without revers.

- Black patent leather shoes.

- A silk top hat or an opera hat.

- Gloves of white buckskin when outdoors.

- Black socks made of silk or nylon.

- Black shoes without toe caps. Shoes may be patent leather or fine, thin leather with a high polish.

Optional:

- Overcoat of black, very dark blue, or Oxford grey smooth cloth (not tweed), with or without a velvet collar.

- Scarf. White silk is the most traditional. (Sometimes scarves are monogrammed in black, white, or grey.)

Jewelry

Traditional men's jewelry is simple and functional no matter what the occasion. A wedding band and/or simple signet ring may be worn but not diamonds or other glittering stones including light-colored stones, rubies, or emeralds. The traditional choice is plain gold without chasing or decorations. Traditional signet rings may be set with a flat semiprecious stone and the gold or stone surface may be engraved or cut with a monogram, family crest, or coat of arms.

Classic cuff links or stud sets for evening are gold or platinum or a combination of both, but cuff links and studs set with single, small cabochon-cut sapphires or amethysts are acceptable on formal occasions.

The traditional shirt studs worn with white tie are made of pearl. Waistcoat studs may be mother-of-pearl, gold, or covered with the material of the waistcoat. Cuff links, shirt, and waistcoat studs often match but it is not necessary that they do.

Wrist watches are never worn with a formal dress suit.

Handkerchiefs

Plain white handkerchiefs are worn with formal evening clothes. Any monogram should be white. Shake the handkerchief and fold loosely before you place it in your breast pocket. Avoid carefully arranged points.

Boutonnieres

A small flower called a boutonniere may be worn by a man with evening attire. However, the boutonniere should be fresh and never artificial. The most usual flower for a man to wear with a black or midnight blue jacket is a small white or dark red carnation. Blue cornflowers (bachelor's-buttons) are popular with white jackets. White boutonnieres may be worn with white tie. Other small flowers or tight flower buds may be worn.

"The automobile changed our dress, manners, social customs, vacation habits, the shape of our cities, consumer purchasing patterns, common tastes ..."

John Keats, 1958
The Insolent Chariots

CAR COURTESY

Automobiles are a part of every day living. Knowing how to gracefully enter and exit a car as well as how to help others into and out of vehicles can keep this everyday exercise from being awkward. Not every day will you be wearing jeans and scrambling into the family car.

While entering the front seat of most vehicles is the same, entering the back seat of a two-door car is not.

Entering and Exiting

Entering a car with a standard door
Stand with your back to the seat once the door is open. Lower your body to the seat keeping your back to the seat. Next, lift your legs holding them together and turning your body to face the front of the car. You'll not only look graceful, but you will prevent ripping your clothes.

Exiting a car with a standard door
Once the door is open, turn your body to face the open door. Place your legs together and lift them out of the car onto the ground.

Entering the back seat of a two-door car

Bend your body into the open door and first place one leg inside once the door is open and the front seat pushed back. (If you are entering the right side of the car, put your left leg in first or your right leg if you are entering the left side of the car.) Once your body is inside the car, turn yourself to face the front and lower yourself to the edge of the seat while pulling the remaining leg into the car.

Exiting the back seat of a two-door car

Turn your body towards the open door once the door is open and the front seat pushed back. Lift the foot nearest the door and place it on the ground. Use the foot remaining in the car to push your body headfirst from the car.

Helping Into and Out of Automobiles

- A man opens the car door to seat a woman.

- Women enter the curbside of the car first and the man walks around to the other side of the car after helping the woman enter the car. When the driver side of the car is exposed to dangerous traffic the man gets into the car first and slides over followed by the woman. (Common sense prevails. The man dressed in trousers will have an easier time sliding over than a woman who is wearing a dress.) The woman may enter the car first when both are wearing trousers. The man who practices social etiquette and has gotten into the car first may offer to close the door by saying to the woman, "May I reach over and close the door?"

Today, this social etiquette occurs most often when the woman is wearing a nice dress or formal clothing. It is also acceptable for the woman to close the door as it is closer to her.

• It is correct for men to offer a woman assistance, but it is never correct for him to force this courtesy on her.

• A man offers his hand palm up to help the woman.

• A man withdraws his hand as soon as it is no longer needed.

• People sitting on the door side of the car get out of the car whenever occupants sitting in the middle of the seat need to get out of the car.

"If a man be gracious and courteous to strangers, it shows he is a citizen of the world, and that his heart is no island cut off from other lands, but a continent that joins to them."

Francis Bacon, 1625
Of Goodness and Goodness of Name

TRAVEL SAVVY

Flying the Friendly Skies

Recent news accounts lament the serious decline of manners aboard planes. Flight attendants and airline personnel have scores of stories of abusive, rude passengers. Likewise, travelers feel slighted by airline employees. Flights are fraught with unplanned and unexpected behavior. Long lines, delayed flights, lost baggage, catering mistakes – all are compounded when crowds of people are in a hurry. Unfortunately, the flight attendants endure most of the bad behavior. A few tips:

- Avoid using loud, threatening, abusive language toward airline personnel.

- Remember that flight attendants are on board for your safety – they are not like waiters in a restaurant.

- Airlines are in the business of transporting you - not impressing you with fancy meals, snacks or beverages.

- Catering mistakes are not the fault of the flight attendants. This includes forgetting special meals, not having enough entrees, serving entrees you don't like and not having food on board except for pretzels, even if a meal is scheduled.

- No one can control the weather – don't take out your frustrations about canceled flights on airline personnel.

Airplanes have a limited amount of space

- Don't try to bypass baggage claim by toting all of your belongings on the plane and taking more than your share of overhead storage space.

- Avoid strolling down the narrow aisle with too many bags and banging into the other passengers with your bags.

- Stay in your "space" – don't spread your work across the seats or hold your newspaper in your seatmate's face.

- Adhere to airline rules regarding portable computer and cell telephone use.

- Avoid striking up a long, personal conversation with the person sitting next to you. Exchange a few pleasantries, but don't continue to talk to someone if he is trying to work or relax.

- Leave the lavatory spotless. Use a paper towel to wipe around the sink. This is not a place to have a sponge bath.

- Leave your seat area spotless. Properly dispose of napkins, cups, apple cores, newspapers and other papers.

- Say, "Thank you!" to the crew as you deplane.

BODY LANGUAGE

"What you do speaks so loud that I cannot hear what you say."

Ralph Waldo Emerson

Did you know that according to research, 93% of communication is non-verbal and that words account for only 7% of a person's message! Physical appearance contributes to 50% of the first impression and occurs before an individual has spoken. Physical appearance includes every visual aspect including grooming, dress, energy level, and movement. Body language that demonstrates confidence compels people to listen. Facial expression, body posture, position of arms, legs, and feet can convey interest in a conversational partner or reveal anxiety, nervousness, shyness, boredom, or dislike. Effective communicators know spoken words alone are not enough.

Experts agree that people who appear to be the most intelligent and powerful are those who draw the least attention to their hands, legs, feet, and head. The gestures of these people are purposeful.

Unfavorable sitting positions when you are talking to someone include various other positions. Crossing legs over the thigh is commonly called the "know it all" position. A person who sits like this rarely changes his mind especially if he places his hands behind his head. Don't bother trying to bring this person around to your own way of thinking. Straddling a chair as if it were a horse is a typically masculine sitting style. Most people typically view this body position unfavorably as it indicates a forceful and domineering manner. Women who sit this way want to be recognized as forceful and dominating.

The study of body language has also shown that the smaller the vocabulary of the speaker the greater the use of gesture. Body language indeed speaks when the brain cannot. Body language is difficult to control but an awareness of what your body can unknowingly communicate is perhaps the only key to its control.

The speaker may look away from the person he is speaking to when he is speaking as part of the normal function of collecting one's thoughts. Direct eye contact should last 40-60% of the time with the rest of the time letting the eyes roam around the face from the forehead to cheeks to chin. A speaker to several people at one time divides his time between his listeners.

Certain nonverbal patterns can serve as good indicators of a person's true message whether he intends to send the message or not. Experts also agree that to properly interpret body language, the reader must consider additional environmental clues. The following information is provided to pique your curiosity about body language and to encourage you to consider the messages you are sending with your body as well as what you might discover about your conversational partner.

Meanings of The Most Common Body Language

Arms folded across the chest suggests that the speaker is defensive or in disagreement with the conversational partner. (Note, read body language in clusters of gestures. Crossed arms in a cold environment could simply indicate that the communicator is cold!)

Legs crossed at the ankle or knee is a positive posture for both men and women which indicates that the communicator is relaxed. However, when the communicator swings the crossed leg he appears nervous and ill at ease.

Crossing one leg on top of the other at the thigh thus exposing the sole of the foot makes the communicator appear arrogant and in some cultures is interpreted as rude. This position is known as the "know-it-all."

Scratching the back of the neck may suggest not only that the communicator may have an itch, but that he is uncertain about something being discussed.

Blinking the eyes ten times or less per minute indicates boredom while fourteen or more blinks shows nervousness and/or stress, or attraction to another person.

Averting the eyes is usually a sure sign of deceit, guilt or lying.

Raised brows coupled with closed eyes for a moment longer than normal sends the message that the communication partner finds something distasteful and surprising.

Ear pulling, eye rubbing, nose rubbing, chin rubbing, and covering the mouth are interpreted by people who read body language to indicate concealment of information, uncertainty, or an untruth being spoken by the communicator. Read body language in gesture clusters and consider the setting and the individual. For example, the person rubbing his eyes and rubbing his nose may be demonstrating an allergic reaction to the cat in the room not that he is hiding information from someone and cannot look at them. The person covering his mouth may be tired and not intentionally conveying "I shouldn't say that." The social yawn on the other hand can indicate more than fatigue. Often this person is trying to buy extra time when facing a mildly stressful situation. And finally, even when a person wants to appear to be concentrating on a communicator's message by resting the chin with one hand he is in fact conveying boredom.

Public grooming including rearranging the hair is a reassuring habit that boosts self-confidence. The message to anyone watching is that the person feels good about himself. However, while patting the hair or tossing it back implies that the speaker thinks positively about personal appearance, the habit of twirling strands of hair indicates confusion, uncertainty and nervousness. Running a hand through the hair generally conveys a sense of being not sure of what to say or do next.

Note: All grooming should take place out of the public eye.

Stroking the Chin is a promising sign that means the listener is interested.

Showing the hands palms up indicates an open and receptive communicator.

Steepling the fingers, the gesture of pressing the fingers together and resting the fingertips on the chin or mouth, indicates deep thought as though the communicator is praying for an answer.

Tugging at the collar is an indicator that the communicator's body temperature has increased. True, it might be hot in the room and that does need to be considered, but the person who knows how to read nonverbal communication is also aware that body temperature increases when people lie. A hand automatically reaching up to let air in by loosening the collar is truly demonstrating that a person is hot under the collar.

Stroking the necktie is a nonverbal signal that the communicator is trying hard to please and is desirous of making a good impression.

Shoving hands into a shirt, blouse, jacket or pocket is thought to indicate that the communicator is secretive and may not want to communicate. After all, hands thrust deep into the pockets are not available for shaking hands or for any other form of tactile communication. Preoccupation with money (either too much or not enough) is another interpretation when the hand in the pocket jingles money.

Jiggling the foot back and forth when the legs are crossed, tapping the foot on the floor, and drumming the fingers on the table indicate an attempt by the body to run from the setting ... parts of the body are already running away! This communicator is very likely nervous or bored.

Fidgeting with shirts' cuffs or jewelry on the wrists is a signal for a need for attention.

Holding hands or objects in front of the body such as a book or magazine indicates an anxious person desiring a communication barrier. Pulling objects from a briefcase or purse when entering a room gives the message that the person is not prepared and/or stalling for time.

Spreading out when sitting is a gesture that sends off unfavorable messages for both men and women, though the unfavorable message is different for each sex. The man who sits spreading out is signaling that he is taking over, while men interpret a woman who is spreading out as overstepping her bounds. However, if she places only one arm on a nearby chair the nonverbal message is that she wants to be perceived as having equal authority.

Using The Hands to Make Conversation Points

The hands can be quite effective in communicating ideas. Pointing the finger at any one in any culture is likely to generate bad feelings. However, the fingers can be used effectively to reinforce communication that contains numerous items.

Conversation that includes several points can be made easier to follow by using the fingers. Try to keep oral lists to three items as more than three increases the difficulty of oral comprehension. North Americans begin the count with the index finger, followed by the middle finger and ring finger. Europeans typically begin counting with the thumb followed by the index finger and middle finger.

FUNERALS

Every moment of your life will not be happy. Inevitably, people you know will get sick or struck by tragedy and some day die. Ignoring sickness, death and moments of sadness will not make them go away. However, knowing what to expect and how to respond during unhappy times will help you and those who need you.

What to do to Help the Grieving

Let those who are grieving know that you care about them and are sorry for their loss. It is painful to experience the death of someone special. Sadness can be compounded when others who care remain silent and do nothing. Not expressing sympathy may be interpreted by those who are mourning as a sign that no one cares. You can let those who are mourning know that you care in several ways.

Sympathy Visits

When someone dies the feeling of loss often seems overwhelming. Friends and family who rally around the grieving can be a big help. It is greatly appreciated if you can visit the grieving at their home. Your presence is a show of support and lets them know that they are not alone. Close friends often help in many ways such as answering the telephone and the door, preparing meals, and keeping a record of visitors and any food or flowers that are received. Sometimes the family prefers to see people at the funeral home or at the church. Look in the news obituary for this option.

You will want to visit during the seven days after the funeral if your friend is Jewish and the custom of sitting shivah is practiced. (The time before the funeral is generally a time for family to be together.)

Listen to your grieving friend when he wants to talk. Being present when a grieving person needs to talk is important. It is not necessary for you to talk when your friend is trying to find / sort out answers. Being present to listen is what he needs from you. Be sincere when you speak and avoid cliches such as "He is at peace now," and references to religion that the bereaved may not share or appreciate. Do say the deceased person's name and share memories. Repeating humorous stories about the deceased will often lighten the sadness.

Notes of Condolence

Letting those who are sad know that you care is very comforting. Many stores sell sympathy cards, but the most personal notes are those that are handwritten. The most traditional condolence notes are handwritten in black ink on formal letter sheets. (See the section on correspondence for details.) Write what you truly feel. Be sincere. Let the person know that you are sorry and that you care. Do write about anything you remember about the person who has died that made that person special or unique. Funny stories are okay, as in "I loved the way he always sang off key at the caroling parties." Avoid formal or flowery language or saying things like "It was a blessing in disguise," "She wouldn't want you to cry and be sad," or other phrases that try to minimize the loss. The person you are comforting needs to know simply that you care. Therefore, it is not necessary to write a long note.

Example of a Sympathy Note

Dear George,

I am so sorry to learn of your dad's death. He was one of my favorite people. I'll never forget the fun time he took us camping at River's Edge, helped us build a huge bonfire, and then led us in singing around the campfire. I'll miss him. You and your family are in my thoughts and prayers. Please let me know if there is anything I can do.

Your friend,
Joe

Telephone Calls of Sympathy

You may choose to telephone to express your sympathy. However, remember that visitors will likely be at the home immediately after the death and that it could be inconvenient to tie up the telephone lines. Close family members unable to attend the funeral will of course want to telephone right away. However, remember that it is often a better idea to wait until your friend can have an uninterrupted conversation with you when the home is not so busy.

Food

Family and friends gathered appreciate food. If you are a close friend, you might consider preparing a dish for them.

Flowers

In the United States, it is a Christian custom to send flowers to the home of the deceased, the place of worship or to the funeral home unless the obituary requests that no flowers be sent. Sign accompanying cards with your first and last names. If you learn of the death after the funeral, it is acceptable to send flowers late. In fact in the Islamic culture, flowers should be sent after the funeral. Be aware that some religions and cultures have customs regarding flowers. For example, in France, chrysanthemums symbolize mourning and in Japan, the color white symbolizes death. Traditional Jewish custom views flowers as a joyful expression so it is preferable to express sympathy in other ways to those grieving families.

Donations to Charities

Sometimes the family prefers that no flowers be sent. This is indicated in the newspaper obituary by the phrase "in lieu of flowers a donation may be sent to..." A donation in the approximate amount of an arrangement of flowers is appropriate. Send the donation directly to the designated charity (not to your friend) along with a note indicating the name of the person the gift is in memory of and the address of the bereaved so the family can be notified. Donations to other charities are appropriate especially if a specific charity has not been designated for memorials.

Keep in Touch

After the funeral, your friend will continue to be sad. Demonstrate your support of your friend by periodically calling or visiting. The first holiday of their loved ones death will be especially difficult as will be the first holidays without the special person. They will appreciate your kindness. Invite your friend out and offer to accompany your friend to the cemetery.

What To Do And Expect When Someone Close To You Dies

This will be one of the hardest events you will ever experience. No one can prepare you for the way you will feel. Everyone feels differently. Knowing that other people care will comfort you. You can expect family and friends to visit, telephone and to do nice things for you. Accept the love and support of other people that will not only help you but also helps them work through their own process of grieving. People will not expect you to carry on conversations or feel like doing many of the things you usually do. Do participate as you feel you are able, and say "thank you" when others show kindness. Take care of yourself.

After the funeral/memorial service, you and your family will probably feel extremely tired and sad for a long time. It may take a long time for you to feel happy again. The length of time is different for everyone. Your family and friends will offer support but if your grief is overwhelming, you may want to get professional help from a priest or counselor.

Acknowledgement of Sympathy

When life begins to return to normal, one of the first things you will want to do is thank those who sent food, flowers, gave donations to charities, wrote personal notes of condolence or expressed their sympathy in other special ways. A simple thank you note from you or a close family member will be appreciated. The note need not be long, but it should be handwritten. Traditional thank you notes for a personal expression of sympathy are written on fold-over notes. Courtesy notes are often supplied by funeral homes but use personal fold-over notes if you have them. Engraved or printed cards are appropriate to send to acknowledge impersonal messages of sympathy which are too numerous to thank with a personal note. It is not necessary to write to those who sent sympathy cards with no personal message or to those who visited the funeral home.

Appropriate Clothing

Gone are the days when black clothing was the only acceptable color to be worn when mourning. However, subdued colors and clothing that does not attract attention is appropriate. Those in mourning generally receive many visitors who come to offer support and show respect. One way visitors show respect is by wearing nice clothing. Those grieving need to dress accordingly to receive these visitors. Adults typically wear dark suits and dresses to funerals. Young children wear their best clothes.

DINING SKILLS

"The world was my oyster 'til I used the wrong fork."

Oscar Wilde

You may forever enjoy and encounter simple, casual meals. This section will prepare you for those meals as well as elaborate multi-course dinners. Read all of the information in this chapter now instead of waiting for a formal occasion to arrive. You never know when you might unexpectedly be presented with lots of utensils, an array of glasses, and unusual foods. Be prepared and you'll feel confident in any situation.

AT THE TABLE

SEATING

A man accompanying a woman to dinner helps to seat her. He does this by holding the top of the chair with both hands and pulling the chair out from the table. The woman enters the chair from the right side, sits on the edge and places her hands on the side of the chair. The man gently pushes the chair forward while the woman adjusts her seat. The man enters his chair from the right and seats himself so that the woman is seated on his right.

Sit in the chair with comfortable straight posture. Lean slightly forward when eating. Arms and elbows should not be on the table when food is on the table. It is acceptable to place elbows on the table when no food is on the table and you are in a noisy restaurant and must lean far forward to be heard by your dining companion. Avoid tipping your chair back as you might fall as well as ruin the furniture!

The man who seats a woman at a table should rise to help her if she leaves the table briefly during the meal. His gesture is usually only a half-rise. If a man is seated on either side of her, only the man seated to her left is expected to assist her.

When the meal is concluded, the man exits his chair from the right side, pushes his chair back to the table and then assists the same woman he helped seat exit the table. He does this by standing behind her chair and helping her to gently slide the chair away from the table. The woman will correctly exit her chair from the right side. The man will push her chair back in to the table so it will be out of the way.

American style dining requires that hands remain in the lap except when using silverware. European style dining requires that the hands remain in view at the table with the wrists touching the edge of the table except when lifting food to the mouth.

THE BLESSING

The custom of saying grace or giving thanks for food generally precedes the meal in the United States. Some people choose to stand for the blessing, others remain seated for the blessing, while others may choose to hold hands while giving thanks. Guests should follow the lead of their hosts. A guest who does not share the same faith is not expected to participate in this religious moment. However, the good guest will show respect by being still and silent at this time. In public places, most diners give thanks silently especially when they are part of a group of diners of mixed religions. A family dining out together may choose to express thanks aloud.

NAPKINS AND WAITING

The minutiae of dining etiquette dictates that guests not touch anything on the table until the host gives one of several silent signals. The host does not give this signal until after water is served to everyone. At that point, the host places his napkin (located on the service plate in front of him or to the left of his plate) on his lap. Napkin

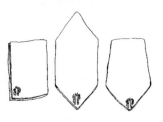

rings are usually used in homes for family gatherings where linen napkins may be used more than once. If you do find your napkin in a ring, remove the napkin and place the ring to the left of your plate. Do not shake the napkin out flamboyantly like a magician, although sometimes a waiter seating you may flap a napkin into your lap that has been placed in the glass at your place setting. If the napkin is a large dinner napkin, (22 to 24 inches square or larger), pick it up with the left hand and place it on your lap so that a single fold faces the lap. Smaller luncheon size napkins are completely unfolded and placed in the lap. Paper napkins are treated the same as cloth napkins. Unless you are less than five years old or are eating lobster, the napkin is never tied around the neck. The napkin is never tucked into trousers, and neckties are not tucked into shirts. Men leave jackets on when dining.

The napkin stays on the lap throughout the meal except when periodically lifted to blot the mouth. Pick up the napkin if you drop a napkin on the floor in someone's home. You may continue using it or ask your host for a new napkin. Leave your dropped napkin on the floor at a restaurant and ask the wait staff for a clean napkin as this is part of the duty of the staff.

At the conclusion of the meal, the host will signal the end by placing his loosely folded napkin to the left of his plate. At this point guests place their loosely folded napkins (soiled portion facing down) to the left of their own plates. (Never push your plate towards the center of the table to indicate that you have finished. The only dish at the table you should ever reposition is the finger bowl.)

It is rude to leave the table unless necessary. Your absence will cause a conversation gap. If you must excuse yourself, you do not need to apologize, ask, or make an announcement. Simply say to those within immediate earshot, "Excuse me." Exit your chair from the right, place your napkin in your seat, and tuck your chair into the table out of the way of restaurant traffic. The napkin in the chair is a silent signal to the wait staff that you will return to the table. Sometimes wait staff will move your napkin onto the arm of the chair or return it to the left of your plate as a silent signal to you that you continue to be looked after while you are away from the table. The attentive waiter will note a badly soiled napkin and replace your napkin with a fresh one if necessary. He lets you know that he has checked your napkin during your absence by repositioning your napkin.

It is courteous for a man to assist the woman seated to his right when she excuses herself from the table and later returns. The man may stand or half rise to help the woman move her chair away from the table. A woman typically does not assist the man seated to her left when he leaves and returns from the table although an offer of help to anyone who needs it is good manners. The person who leaves the table is careful to push the chair back in to the table to keep it out of the way of wait staff or other guests passing by the table.

You are likely to see people you know when you dine in a public restaurant. It is polite to acknowledge them, but in a non-intrusive way. First, if someone you know stops by your table to say hello, it is courteous for you to stand and remain standing until he leaves. Standing shows self-respect and respect for the other person.

If you are the visitor at someone's table remember not to linger or engage in lengthy conversation. You are most certainly interrupting another's dining experience. Often you will hear an interloper say, "Please keep your seat," but this is rude because if the person follows the request he will appear to be a dolt.

BEVERAGES AT THE TABLE

Guests wait for the host to offer drinks before ordering drinks in a restaurant. Remember the following when drinks are served with stirrers and garnishes:

- Remove stirrers (stirrers are not meant to be used as mini straws.)

- Remove decorations like umbrellas.

- Stir tea with a spoon without making a clinking sound.

- Remove the iced teaspoon or other spoon from a glass or cup before drinking. Place the spoon on the saucer beneath the glass or cup. The spoon is placed behind the glass or cup with handle to the right. If a saucer is not available ask for one or use one of your available plates. (Used utensils are never placed directly on the table).

- Add sugar to the beverage with a sugar spoon and do not place the serving spoon in your glass or cup. Ask for a serving spoon if one is not in the community sugar bowl. (You may use your own spoon only if you have not used it.)

- Do not place sugar wrappers in an ashtray. Fold the wrappers and place under the side of the saucer.

- Lemons, limes, cherries etc. are garnishes. Remove them or float them in your drink. Do not squirt lemon or lime wedges in your glass and risk shooting someone in the eye. If you simply must have the juice from a lemon wedge, be sure to shield it with the other hand when squeezing. Lemon slices usually served with hot tea are only for floating.

- Ice is for chilling drinks, not for crunching and chewing.

EATING ETIQUETTE

- Do not begin to eat until everyone at your table has been served. Wait for the hostess to lift her fork before you begin.

- You may begin to eat when those around you have been served if you are seated at a long banquet table where many people are eating.

- Chew with your mouth closed, keep your arms close to your body when you eat.

- Chew and swallow the food in your mouth, then wipe your lips with your napkin before talking or drinking from a glass.

- Use designated serving pieces, not the silverware from your place setting, to serve yourself from main dishes such as meat, vegetable, butter or sugar. Ask your host or waiter for any needed serving utensils.

- Instead of reaching across the table for something, ask the person closest to the dish or item you want to pass it to you. Asking a specific person keeps others at the table from looking about for your request.

- Cut your food into bite-sized pieces one bite at a time.

- Use a knife to cut salad, vegetables, and meat—do not use the side of your fork.

- Break your bread into bite-sized pieces and butter the bread one bite at a time.

- Place your knife and fork side-by-side and far enough from the edge of the plate so they won't fall off when passing your plate for a second helping.

- Elbows should not be on the table while you are eating. Elbows may be on the table when no food is on the table between courses.

- Avoid leaning on chairs placed beside you and tilting back your chair. More than one chair has been broken by a person tilting his chair back at the table.

- Pace your eating to match that of the other diners.

- Never eat and run!

TOASTING

Toasting may occur at any time during the meal in the United States but typically is offered towards the end of the meal.

Toasts may be made for multiple reasons such as to welcome, to say goodbye, or to congratulate. The one rule is that you must have a beverage in order to toast. Water may be used for toasting, but some people think it is bad luck to toast with water. Use only three fingers to lift a water or wine glass, two fingers to lift a champagne flute. Avoid the affectation of sticking out your pinky.

The English coined the word toast to describe the "drinking a health" custom. Wine of old had a great deal of sediment. A piece of toast was placed in the glass to absorb the sediment. Local legend in Bath, England is that some admirers scooped water from the bath of a woman enjoying the local water and used it to drink to her health. According to Richard Steele in the *1709 Tatler*, one of the admirers said that "tho' he liked not the Liquor (water), he would have the Toast." The word toast in the English language has been used to describe the act of drinking to one's health or drinking in honor of someone since those early days in Bath, England.

The person giving a toast must be seen by all. Stand when offering a formal toast. (You may remain seated when proposing an informal toast at a single, small table.) Hold the glass at eye level in the direction of the person being toasted. Keep your toast brief. Mark Twain advised that "thirty seconds is really long enough to say anything worth saying and that any toasts except my own should never last longer than a minute!" When you finish speaking, take a sip from your drink. It is an added honor if all other guests rise, raise their glasses in the direction of the honored person, and then drink. Not to participate in a toast to someone is rude so even if you don't want to drink, at least lift the glass to your lips in the spirit of participation.

The person being toasted remains seated while everyone sips the toast. Afterwards he picks up his glass and gestures to the person or group toasting him. The recipient of the toast does not drink to himself, but says "thank you" as a toast is a compliment. The recipient of the toast may raise his glass after the toast to him and say, "And to good friends!" Recipients of toasts should return the toasts either immediately after receiving a toast or later during the dining event usually preceding or during dessert. The length of this toast should not exceed the length of the host's toast.

Avoid the archaic custom of clinking glasses together when drinking a toast. The owner of the glasses will appreciate your courtesy. The old habit of clinking glasses had to do with fears of poison and superstition.

THE FORMAL PLACE SETTING

The elements of the formal place setting from left to right.

Fish fork, dinner fork, salad fork, place plate/service plate/charger with napkin and place card. (The service plate, a luncheon-sized plate, is identical to the place plate, a dinner-sized plate, except it is smaller and most often used at buffet tables. Both are made only of porcelain. Food may be eaten from the service and place plates. A charger differs from the service and place plates in that it is the largest of the three and may be made of any material including wood, metal, or porcelain. Food is never eaten from a charger. The charger may be correctly placed under a place or service plate and is not removed until the main course is served.) Salad knife, dinner knife, fish knife, soup spoon with oyster fork resting in its bowl. Above the forks: A bread and butter plate with butter spreader.

Above the bread and butter plate is an individual pepper pot and salt cellar.

Above the place plate: dessert ware including dessert knife, fork, and spoon.

Above the dessert ware is the menu card.

Above the knives: The glasses from left to right, water glass, red wine glass, white wine glass, and sherry glass. The champagne tulip glass is behind and to the right of the water goblet.

Four Basic Dining Styles

Four basic dining styles are practiced throughout the world today: American (zigzag), Continental (European), Asian, and Communal (with the hands). No one style is better than another is. The style is simply different. Respect various eating styles as you respect the people using the different styles. Further, be aware that even though the continental style is perfectly correct, in many parts of the United States the use of the Continental style may be misinterpreted as the use of bad manners by those who do not know any better!

Whatever style you choose, practice it correctly.

The elements of the American and European place setting are usually the same. However, you may find some subtle variations in the Continental style place setting when dining in Europe and in some places in the United States. The primary difference is the orientation of the fork and spoon. In the Continental style the tines of the fork and the bowl of the spoon may be placed face down so that the handle's engraving or silver marks are visible. In the American style, the silverware is placed upward and the handle markings are not showing. In addition, the cheese knife and dessert fork or spoon are placed above the plate. The casual Continental style place setting may offer only one knife per place setting. This knife is intended to be used for more than one course. Note that at the most formal meal no more than thirteen pieces of silver appear on the table at one time. Additional pieces are brought in as needed.

Traditionally, a single plate was used at each place setting and was replaced after each course. In the formal place setting illustration, note the use of an American invention, a place plate, which is sometimes called a presentation plate or charger. It is now popularly used in formal dining by Americans and Europeans. The place plate remains in front of the diner until the entree arrives. In American dining, entree means main course. In European dining, the French word l'entree designates the appetizer course.

The napkin correctly rests on the place plate. The napkin is correctly placed to the left of the forks if the place plate is not being used. Place the napkin in your lap with the fold to your waist after the host has placed his napkin in his lap.

Beverages

Beverage glasses placed above the silverware to the right of your plate belong to your place setting. Your water glass is the glass that is the farthest to the left and roughly in line with the tip of your main-course knife. The main-course glass is positioned to the right of the water glass and slightly in front of it. When multiple beverages such as wine are served, an additional wineglass may be positioned in one of two ways. First, it may be placed to the right of the water glass with the larger wineglass behind the smaller one, roughly forming a triangle. An alternative position is to place the three glasses from the largest to smallest in a diagonal line down and to the right. A sherry glass or first course wineglass will be located farthest to the right side when offered. The first beverage glass and silverware used are those farthest from the plate.

A glass for chilled beverages such as iced tea, iced coffee, or milk is positioned to the right of the water glass and is not combined with any wineglasses. Long-handled iced-tea spoons with small bowls are made available for the iced drinks to which sugar may be added and are positioned to the far right outside of any knives, spoons, or oyster fork.

Hold long-stemmed water and wineglasses by the thumb and first two fingers at the base of the bowl. Hold small stemmed glasses by the stems. Hold tumblers near the base. Only brandy snifters are held in the palms of both hands.

The following section describes the various place setting components, a step by step description of service during the meal, and how to eat the various foods that may be served during the course using the correct cutlery. Six courses are the maximum for even the most elaborate formal dinner.

The Six Courses are:

First Course: Soup, fresh fruit cup, melon, or shellfish may be presented during the first course.

Second Course: Fish is generally served but sweetbreads or another dish may be served if shellfish is served during the first course.

Third Course: The entree or main course (usually meat or fowl and vegetables.)

Fourth Course: Salad (Salad is often served before the main course in the United States and after the main course in Europe.)

Fifth Course: Dessert

Sixth Course: Coffee

You can anticipate the food and the order it will be served by observing the type and arrangement of the utensils, dishes, and glasses. Read the place setting beginning with the utensils located on the outside because you will use the outer utensils first and as each course is served you will use the succeeding utensils towards the plate. Both lunch and dinner have a typical series of courses or menus. The following list includes those you might expect, but not all the courses described here will necessarily be included at any one meal.

The Appetizer Course

The first course may be served at the table or preceding the meal during a cocktail hour away from the table. In the United States the first course is often referred to as an hors d'oeuvres or appetizer.

Typical first-course dishes are oysters or clams on the half shell, caviar, smoked salmon, prosciutto and melon, and some salads – in small servings. Soup may also be served as a first-course. Traditionally, cut-up fruit is not served as a first-course, but many restaurants have begun to offer it. You can anticipate what your first course might be by looking at the silverware.

If you observe a small fork on the far right of the place setting, you can assume that you will be enjoying some sort of seafood as the first-course. If you see a small and slender fork to the far left, and/or a small and slender knife to the far right, and/or a fruit spoon to the far right, you may anticipate being served fruit as the first course. If a soupspoon appears on the far right, you will be served soup. We will discuss the possibility of seafood first.

Seafood as a First-Course

The small fork with its tines resting in the bowl of the soupspoon is a cocktail fork. (As an alternative it may be simply placed to the far right of the place setting.) It is the only fork correctly placed to the right of the plate. This fork indicates that you will perhaps have a seafood cocktail such as shrimp for the first-course. The cocktail fork, or oyster fork as it is sometimes called, is small with short tines. It is used for clams and oysters on the half-shell, mussels, snails, and lobster in the shell, seafood cocktail, and for serving lemon slices, pickles, etc.

How to Eat Shrimp Cocktail

Shrimp cocktail is usually served in a short stemmed dish containing chipped ice. In the center of the ice will likely be cocktail sauce. Shrimp are often positioned over the dish's rim. Use the small cocktail fork to eat the shrimp. If the shrimp is too large for one bite you may steady the dish with your left hand and cut the shrimp in two with the edge of the fork. Another alternative is to place the very large shrimp on the plate under the shrimp cup and cut it with a knife and fork. Place the knife across the top of the plate as described under Correct Usage of Knife  and Fork. Then pierce the shrimp with the fork and dip only one bite at a time into the sauce. Place the cocktail fork on the plate underneath the dish after each bite. (A fork remaining in the shallow dish may easily be knocked out.) The difficulty of maneuvering very large shrimp sometimes makes it necessary to eat the shrimp one bite at a time from the fork. This is the only exception to the rule of putting only one bite of food on the fork at a time. Lemon wedges may be offered. Spear the wedge with your fork and squeeze it over the shrimp while covering it with your other hand.

How to Eat Raw Oysters and Clams on the Half Shell

To eat raw oysters and clams on the half shell it is necessary to steady the shell on the plate and lift the meat in one piece with the small oyster fork. If you like sauce, you should dip the raw oyster or clam in the sauce and eat it in one bite. In very informal dining, it is acceptable to pick up the shell and pour the juice into your mouth. When oyster crackers are served, do not drop them into cocktail sauce.

How to Eat Steamed Clams and Steamed Mussels

Steamed clams and steamed mussels are served in their semi-opened shells. Fully separate the clam's or mussel's two shells over you plate, discard the half shell without the clam, and then firmly hold the shell containing the meat with the left hand and pull it out by the neck. Pull off the neck sheath, dip the meat first into broth and then into drawn butter which is served in a separate container. Eat the clam in one bite. The neck of the meat is edible if you choose to eat it. Pile the empty shells on the side of your plate using your butter plate if your plate becomes full. Sometimes a waste bowl or second plate will be provided for the discarded shells. You may enjoy drinking the clam broth that is brought to you as a dip for the clams. However, it is not considered polite to drink the clam broth in which the clams are served.

Fruit As a First-Course

Cantaloupe, other melons, or papaya cut in halves or quarters, or grapefruit halves may be served either as a first or last course. Melon, typically the water-melon, served in sections with the rind is eaten with a spoon. Melon is eaten with a fork when the rind is removed. Melon is eaten with a spoon when served in small balls.

Grapefruit Spoon

This spoon has a pointed bowl and is used for eating half a grapefruit or a section of melon. The fruit's juice may be scooped out with the spoon and eaten — except at very formal meals. Do not however, squeeze the fruit at the table to obtain the juice.

The Fruit Knife

The fruit knife may be used at informal meals when whole fruit is served. It is a small, slender knife with a serrated blade.

Soup as a First-Course or Second-Course

Soup may be served as the first-course or it may be served as the second-course at a formal meal. At an informal lunch, substantial soup such as brunswick stew may be served as the main course, in which case it might be accompanied by a salad.

The type of soupspoon will indicate the type of soup you will likely be served. Four different spoons may be used depending on the soup.

- The *place spoon* is larger than a teaspoon. It is used for soup served in a soup plate or bowl, and at other times for cereal, some desserts, or as a small serving spoon.

- The *consommé spoon* has a round bowl and short handle. It is used for soup served in a consommé cup, and at other times for serving certain sauces, jam, jelly, and so on.

- The *cream soupspoon* is similar in size to a place spoon but has a rounded bowl. It is used for cream soup and for the same purposes as a place spoon.

- The *large soupspoon,* is larger than a place spoon, has an oval bowl and is only correctly used for soup served in a soup plate or as a serving spoon.

Formal etiquette suggests specific bowls be used for specific soup at specific times. Modern conventions have provided the diner with all-purpose bowls. These all-purpose bowls may be the ones you most often find at the table. However, in case you are in charge of organizing a special meal and want it served correctly, you need to know the following.

Small soup cups are typically used midday regardless of the type of soup. The exception is when the soup is served as a hearty main course - then it is common sense to use a good-sized bowl such as a soup plate. The larger soup plate is used for serving all hot soups in the evening. Handled cups are used to serve jellied soups and cold cream soups such as Vichyssoise.

Soup is most formally served after the diners are seated. Informally, the soup may already be placed on the table before the guests are seated or served from a tureen at the table by the hostess.

Some regions have special soups that may be enhanced with additional flavorings or toppings. Your hostess will likely pass these toppings around the table after everyone has been served. (Remember, pass to the right.) You might expect sherry with she-crab or turtle soup, tobassco with stews, and shredded cheese, sour cream, diced onions and chives with some chilies.

How To Eat Soup

Spoon the soup away from you. It is correct to tilt the soup plate slightly away from you if necessary to get the soup in the spoon. Sip soup from the side of the spoon. Never put the entire bowl of the spoon into your mouth. The spoon should rest on the right side of the saucer under the consommé cup or cream soup bowl. Never leave your spoon standing in these shallow dishes. The soup plate is larger and can accommodate a spoon resting on its surface.

Crackers may be served with soup. Small oyster crackers or croutons may be placed whole in the soup, but larger crackers are eaten separately and never crumpled into the soup. Place these crackers on your bread and butter plate or on the plate placed beneath the soup bowl. Avoid holding a cracker in one hand and a soupspoon in the other. Eat a bite of the cracker, put it down on the bread and butter plate or plate beneath the soup, and then pick up your soupspoon.

The Fish-Course

Only at very formal dinners are both a fish course and a meat course served. At all other dinners and at lunch, fish, when served, is the main course.

Eating Fish: The Fish Fork and Fish Knife

The fish fork resembles the salad fork in size and design. The tines are broad with light indentations for lifting the skeleton of the fish when it is served with bones. It is placed on the left corresponding with that of the fish knife on the right. How to use the fish fork will be discussed in conjunction with the fish knife.

The fish knife is easy to recognize as it has a wide, dull blade with a notch on the top near the tip of the knife blade. This special knife is used for flaking the fish and guiding it onto the backside of the tines of the fork in order to eat the fish.

In addition, the fish knife is used to separate the halves of a fish when it is served whole.

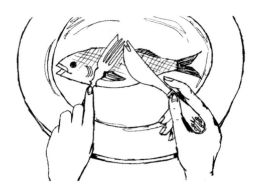

Fish may be served in portions or whole. If you are served a whole fish, you should bone it by first cutting off the head and tail and placing them or one side of the plate. Next, cut the fish between the backbone and the bottom half lifting the backbone and placing it with the head and tail. When correctly cut, the two filets will be boneless. To do this, use the notch on the fish knife to separate the top and bottom halves. Secure the fish with the inverted fish fork in your left hand and with the right hand use the knife to remove the edge of the fish's stomach. Continue along the backbone. Lift the top half of the fish and then eat the boneless half as described. When you are ready for the second half, place the fish knife between the other fish portion and the backbone. Lift the backbone with the fish knife and fork onto the side of your dinner plate or onto a special bone dish if one is provided.

Fish is flaked never cut because it is not tough like meat. To flake fish, use the fish knife with the fish fork in the following manner. Hold the fork in your left hand so that your index finger is pointing down toward the tines of the fork that are facing down. Hold the fish knife in your right hand like a pencil. Secure the fish knife between your pointed index finger and curved middle finger. The handle of the knife correctly rests on the web between your thumb and index finger. Use the fish knife to flake the fish onto the backside of your fork's tines.

Fish bones may be a problem. It is correct to use your fingers to remove fish bones from your mouth. Place the fish bones on the side of your plate or in the fish bone dish at your place setting. The bone dish is a crescent shaped dish set above and slightly to the left of your dinner plate or fish plate if one is used for serving fish . The fish plate is slightly smaller than a dinner plate and is usually embellished with a fish or marine design. Sometimes, a luncheon plate which is smaller than a dinner plate will be used in place of a fish plate.

The Sorbet Course

Sorbet is a frozen fruit juice like sherbet lacking milk solids served in small portions preceding the main course. Its purpose is to cleanse the palate in preparation for the main course. Sorbet is served in a small dish resting on a plate. A spoon will be brought in with the sorbet. Eat the sorbet as you would sherbet, removing any drips from the spoon by sliding it across the rim of the sorbet dish. Rest the spoon on the plate in between bites when you are finished. The sorbet may be presented with a garnish. You may eat the garnish or place it on the underlying plate.

The Main Course or Entrée

The main course is typically called the meat course. The meat course may or may not be preceded by a first course. It is eaten with specific knives and forks depending on the type of meat served.

The Place Knife and Place Fork

The place knife is located closest to your service plate on the right hand side. The placement corresponds with that of the place fork. It is an all-purpose size knife suitable for the main-course meat, poultry, or fish. In addition, it is used for any course when the food requires cutting such as hard cheese served with a salad or raw fruit.

The place fork is an all-purpose size fork suitable for the main course meat, poultry or fish. The place fork is located closest to your service plate on the left-hand side. The placement corresponds with that of the place knife.

The Dinner Knife and Dinner Fork

The dinner knife and dinner fork are used in place of the place knife and place fork at formal meals. The dinner knife is located to the right of the service plate and is the utensil closest to your service plate on the right hand side. Its position corresponds with that of the dinner fork. The dinner knife is like the place knife only sharper and about an inch longer. It is used for cutting all types of meat at a formal meal. The dinner knife may be replaced by a steak knife when a tougher cut of meat is served. The steak knife has a sharper blade than the place knife and dinner knife.

The dinner fork is located to the left of the service plate and is the utensil closest to your service plate on the left hand side. The dinner fork is about an inch longer than the standard place fork. It is used for the main course of a formal meal.

Correct Usage of the Knife and Fork

Correct holding of the silverware is imperative. Try this trick to get the idea of how to correctly hold flatware for cutting food. Place the knife in your right hand and the fork in your left hand. Balance the handle of the knife and fork on your index finger. Now, gently grasp the handles and turn the knife and fork over facing the plate. The index finger of your right hand should be pointing down the blade of the knife and the index finger of the left hand should be pointing down towards the tines of the fork.

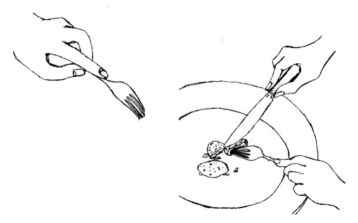

Secure food with the fork and slice with the knife. Do not saw food. Cut only one bite of food at a time. Cutting one bite of food is not only proper etiquette; it also helps to pace the rate of the meal. Further, it is a courtesy to the chef and to those enjoying the chef's appetizing presentation of the food. The tines of the fork and the blade of the knife are always held horizontally over the meat rather than vertically. Never point or gesture with silverware.

At this point the similarities of American and Continental (European) style knife and fork usage ceases. First, let's explore the American style.

The American (Zigzag) Style

After cutting a bite of food, the American style diner rests the knife across the top of the plate with the blade facing inward toward the diner. The fork is then transferred (zigzagged) to the right hand with the fork handle showing between the index finger and thumb (think of holding a pencil). The fork's tines are facing up. Lean slightly forward and lift the food to your mouth while placing your left hand in your lap. Place the empty fork on your plate with the tines facing up in the middle of your plate. The handle of the fork should be resting on the lower right side of your plate. Imagine the face of a clock and rest the fork's handle roughly between four and five o'clock. Silverware should not touch the table once it is used. This includes the handles so avoid dangling utensils from your plate.

The silverware placement just described is known as the "resting position." This position is maintained when you choose to rest in between bites and to listen to conversation. It is also a silent signal to the wait staff that you are still in the process of eating and that your plate should not be removed.

American style dining requires that hands remain in the lap except when using silverware.

Chew with your mouth closed. Do not cut a bite until after chewing and swallowing the current bite. Avoid talking with food in your mouth.

It is good manners to pace your dining with those at your table. Do not rush. The observant host will observe the dining pace and when he notices that all are finished, he will give the silent signal that the present course is finished. The silent signal is again indicated by the placement of the silverware. The silent signal is given by placing the knife and fork handles parallel at the lower right hand corner of the plate at the imagined four and five o'clock place on the plate. The knife is above the fork with the blade facing you and the fork below with the tines facing up. The knife blade and fork tines are in the approximate middle of the plate. This silently signals wait staff to begin removing plates. Staff will remove plates from each diner's right side. Silverware placed in the correct position is a courtesy to the staff because plates can be removed by the waiter by placing the thumb neatly on top of the silverware to secure it while removing the plate.

Note that to place your silverware in the finished position before others are finished sends a nonverbal signal that you are ready to end, so be courteous and politely wait for others before placing your silverware in this position.

The Continental (European) Style

The Continental (European) style diner holds the knife and fork in the position described earlier in cutting the food. The knife remains in the right hand while the fork with tines facing down carries the food to the mouth. Left-handed diners reverse the procedure. The diner may correctly elect to hold the utensils in his hand while chewing each bite and then repeating the process. The diner who continues to hold the utensils while chewing is careful to hold the silverware parallel or pointing slightly down towards the food - not straight up in the air!

The Continental style diner uses a different "resting position" from that used by the American style diner when he chooses to rest between bites, talk, or listen. The correct Continental "resting position" is to rest the knife on the plate first with the blade facing the diner or on a knife rest if one is available. The knife handle is placed at the lower right of the plate between the imagined four and five o'clock. The fork tines rest facing down across the knife on the center of the plate so that the fork's handle is placed at the lower left of the plate. Imagine the face of a clock and rest the fork's handle roughly between seven and eight o'clock. Again, silverware should not touch the table once it is used. This includes the handles so avoid dangling utensils from your plate.

Continental style dining requires that the hands remain visible throughout the meal. Rest the wrists on the table, not the arms and elbows. Apparently, Europeans began this custom because many were suspicious of daggers under the table and the passing of secrets. The visibility of the hands was therefore comforting and courteous. Though the suspicion has disappeared, the tradition continues.

The Continental finished position is the same as the American finished position but the tines are facing down. The finished position is the same for both right and left handed diners in the Continental style.

Bread with the Meal

Bread is typically served with the main course immediately after the meat and vegetables. An entire loaf of bread or individual pieces of bread may be  correctly served. The host or person seated closest to an uncut loaf first slices or breaks off a couple of servings of the bread and passes the breadbasket/cutting board to the person seated to his/her right. The bread is then passed around the table with each man cutting or breaking off a portion for himself and the woman seated to his right. Take only one roll or biscuit when bread is served in individual pieces. Bread is often passed a second time during the meal.

Break all bread before buttering except small biscuits, bite-size sandwiches, and hot homemade country-style biscuits that are sinful not to butter when piping hot! For other breads, break off a bite-sized piece of bread and then butter and eat one bite at a time. The custom of breaking off one small bite at a time is an old courtesy that originated during the days when peasants would be given the food leftover from the table. The thoughtful practice ensured that the leftover bread was as intact as possible when given to the poor.

The Bread and Butter Plate

The bread and butter plate is an American invention and is often simply referred to as the butter plate. It is approximately five inches across and is positioned above the forks and to the left of your dinner plate. Each plate is set with its own butter spreader (small, smooth bladed knife) resting either across the top of the butter plate with its blade facing the diner, or resting across the right hand side of the butter plate with the blade facing towards the plate's center. Traditionally, butter plates were used only for luncheons and informal dinners and were not correct at very formal dinners where the bread was placed directly onto the tablecloth. The butter plate's use has evolved to acceptance at the formal dinner table.

Butter may already be placed on your butter plate or it may be more formally served at the same time as the bread and right after it. When it is served to you in small pats or balls, it is often served with a small pointed fork.

When butter is served to you as a large mold or stick, the butter is served with a butter knife (sometimes called butter server) which is kept at all times on the butter plate with its handle facing to the right and slightly clear of the plate's edge to keep the handle clean. Use this butter knife, not your own

butter spreader, to place the butter on your butter plate. Never put butter from the serving dish directly onto your bread. Place it first on your plate with the butter server and then use your own knife (individual butter spreader if available, dinner knife if individual butter spreader is not made available) to butter your bread.

Pats of butter are sometimes served in individual wrappers. Remove the butter from the wrapper with your knife and place it on your butter plate. Fold the wrapper and place it on the side of the bread plate or under the plate's edge.

Butter the bite of bread you have broken one bite at a time and be sure to hold the bread on or just above the plate. Never hold bread in the palm of your hand, in the air, or flat on the table. Use your fork to take butter from your butter plate to spread on vegetables, potatoes, and corn cut from the cob. Use your knife to butter corn on the cob.

The Salad Course

Salad may be served before, after, or with the main course. The traditional serving of salad is after the main course because the vinegar in the dressing can affect the taste of wine accompanying the main course. In Europe and in most formal restaurants it is served after the main course. The notion of serving the salad before the main course began in California in the 1950s - perhaps to stave off the hunger of impatient diners and to give the cooks more time. The custom of serving the salad before the main course is often called, "California style." The custom of serving salad after the main course is called,

"Continental style." The salad is correctly served bite-sized no matter the service order.

The salad may be served on a separate plate at the same time as the main course. In this instance, your salad plate will be the one located preferably to the left of the main course plate and the forks to its left, or if space between diners is tight, the salad plate may be placed above the forks. Eat your salad from that plate with your salad fork and do not transfer the salad to the dinner plate. Sometimes there is no separate plate for the salad and the salad is placed on one side of the dinner plate and eaten with the main-course fork.

The Salad Fork

Salad forks are medium sized forks positioned on the table either to the left of the dinner fork if salad is served after the main course, or positioned to the right of the dinner fork if the salad precedes the main course. Salad forks are also used for first courses, fish, eggs, pastry, and other desserts.

Sometimes the lettuce leaves the diner is given are not bite-sized and must be cut with a salad knife or dinner knife. The original etiquette was to use only the fork to fold the leaves into a nice little envelope sized bite. Knives were never used for cutting salad in the past. Originally, blades of knives were made of steel, not stainless steel. Acidity from salad dressing would tarnish the knife's blade. With the advent of stainless steel blades, salad knives were created.

The Salad Knife

The salad knife is a medium sized smooth bladed knife which may be correctly positioned to the right or left of the larger dinner knife depending on whether the salad is served before or after the main course.

If the lettuces in your salad are unwieldy and a salad knife is not available, you may use your meat knife to cut the lettuces. (It will later be necessary to ask your waiter for an additional knife unless you keep the meat knife by placing it on your bread and butter plate.) When your salad is served with the main course, it is perfectly correct to use the dinner fork and knife for both.

Directions for using the salad knife and salad fork are the same as using the dinner knife and dinner fork.

The Cheese Course

Some hosts, especially in the United States, choose to serve cheese with the salad. Others, especially Europeans, like to serve it when salad follows the main course. Use your knife to place the cheese on your salad plate when the salad is served with cheese.

Some restaurants enjoy a glorious production of serving cheese and have special staff who are so knowledgeable about the different types of cheese that they are known as a fromager if male and a fromagere if female. These special servers will present an array of cheeses and inform you about which cheeses go best with the wine you are drinking. You make your selections and the fromager will serve you on a separate cheese plate. Eat the cheese with your knife and fork beginning with the milder selections and progressing to the stronger ones. You may eat the cheese with bread or crackers using your knife to spread cheese on one cracker or piece of bread at a time. However, fromagers advise that to fully appreciate the full flavor of cheese, cheese should be eaten alone.

The Dessert Course

Dessert is traditionally served as the last course of the meal in the United States and is usually a sweet dish. (Note that it is usual to combine the service of coffee with the dessert. Some people prefer to enjoy coffee alone and present it after dessert.) However, many Americans and Europeans prefer fresh fruit as the final course. We will discuss eating a sweet dessert first and conclude with the eating of various types of fresh fruit.

The dessert fork, dessert knife, and dessert spoon are both approximately one inch longer than a standard teaspoon. These utensils may be used individually or together, depending on the dessert. Dessert utensils may be presented in two ways.

First, when eating informal meals, the dessert fork, knife and/or spoon may be preset above your dinner plate with the knife closest to the plate and parallel to the edge of the table. The handle of the knife is positioned to the right and the tip of the blade to the left. The blade faces the table's edge. The fork is positioned with the tines up facing the right of the plate with its handle to the left. The spoon is above the fork, bowl facing up, with its handle to the right. More formally, dessert utensils are brought in with the dessert. You may need to use one or all of the utensils. Depending on the dessert, the fork may be used for eating and the spoon as a pusher. Sometimes it is useful to use the fork to secure a slippery dessert by holding it in the left-hand tines down into the dessert such as one that may be frozen. The spoon, held in the right hand, can then spoon into the dessert. Apple pie is eaten with a fork. Apple pie a la mode (with ice cream) is eaten with a spoon.

Dessert may be presented in one of two ways after the table is cleared. The first method is for the server to place a dessert plate with or without a finger bowl on it in front of each diner. (See section How To Use A Finger Bowl.) Afterwards, the server passes the dessert in a large serving dish to each guest.

The second method is to place an already served dessert plate in front of each guest. Ice cream is correctly served in a sherbet glass resting on a dessert plate. (Cookies, etc. served with the ice cream are correctly passed separately. Take a cookie from the main serving plate with your fingers and place it on your plate - not directly into your mouth. Eat a small cookie in one bite, but break a larger one into two pieces.) Dessert silver is brought in on the dessert plate unless it is already on the table as described above. Do not be confused if more dessert silver is brought in than appears to be needed. Some chefs like to present each course in what many perceive as an aesthetic way. Aestheticians balance the presentation of the food in every way including the symmetry of the silverware.

How to Eat Apples and Pears

Quarter apples and pears with a knife, peel the skin off if you choose, core, and eat with your fingers.

How to Eat Grapes and Cherries

Eat grapes and cherries completely using your hand. Note: break off a branch of grapes - not single grapes when you serve yourself from a fruit tray. Sometimes grape shears are placed beside the fruit tray for this purpose.

How to Eat Peaches, Plums, and Nectarines

Eat these fruits with your hands by first cutting the fruit in half, removing the stone, and finally, if you choose, removing the skin.

How to Eat Oranges

Peel oranges with the fruit knife and eat by sections or by half sections if the sections are large.

How to Eat Bananas

Bananas eaten at the table are completely peeled, placed on a plate, and cut into pieces or sliced and eaten with a fork. Save the monkey style for outdoor picnics and the hiking trail.

How to Eat Berries

Strawberries are the only berries not properly eaten solely with a spoon. Strawberries served with the hull are held by the stem and may be dipped in powdered sugar (from your plate, not the sugar dish) and eaten in a bite. Stems and hulls are placed on your plate.

The Finger Bowl

Finger bowls are seldom used anymore, but because they may be used when you are participating in a formal dining occasion you need to know how to use them to prevent embarrassment. One of my favorite stories about finger bowls involves a state dinner at The White House. President George Herbert Walker Bush was hosting a foreign dignitary at a formal meal. When the finger bowls arrived, the foreign dignitary picked up his bowl and drank from it. The guests were anxious wondering what to do. President Bush immediately picked up his finger bowl and drank from it. President Bush realized the importance of helping someone "save face" and demonstrated excellent manners by doing so. He knew the correct finger bowl etiquette, but wisely opted not to embarrass his guest. You can be certain that his guest recognized President Bush's good manners and that Bush's face saving gesture had a positive impact on foreign business relations.

How to Use a Finger Bowl

The finger bowl is generally used after eating foods that cannot be entirely eaten with utensils. For example, it is often used after eating some shellfish, corn on the cob, and perhaps asparagus. Finger bowls are small bowls filled about two-thirds with tepid water. A slice of lemon may be floating in the dish on the occasion that shellfish has been served. The chef may choose to decorate (unnecessarily) by floating a sprig of  mint, a small flower or flower petals, or an aromatic leaf in the finger bowl.

Finger bowls may be brought to the table in one of two ways. First, they may be brought in on the dessert plates (usually resting on a doily and sometimes appearing on an under plate) and placed before the diner. If dessert silverware is not already on the table, the dessert fork will be resting on the left of the dessert plate and the dessert spoon will be resting on the right side of the dessert plate. (Sometimes both utensils are placed on the plate for the sake of balance although both utensils are not necessary.) Each diner then removes the silverware from the dessert plate and places it on the table to the correct left and right positions. Next, if a doily is being used, the diner lifts the doily and bowl in one movement off the dessert plate and places them above and slightly to the left of his place setting. (If the finger bowl arrives on its own under plate it is removed with the finger bowl in one motion.) Follow your hosts' cue if you are not sure.

After each diner has repositioned the finger bowl, his dessert will be placed on the dessert plate. A waiter will not remove the dessert plate after dessert has been eaten. The diner must move the dessert plate to the top of his place setting area so that he has room to replace the dessert plate with the finger bowl. The diner lifts the finger bowl along with its under plate or doily in one motion and places them in front of him. He then dips the fingertips of first one hand and then the other lightly in the water and wipes them on the napkin. The mouth should never be wetted from a finger bowl.

How to Eat Difficult Foods

Avoid ordering foods that you have never eaten before when you are dining with people you do not know well. Observe your host when you are served foods that you do not know how to eat. Read the following pointers on how to eat some of the foods requiring a little extra finesse.

Artichokes: The leaves of artichokes are pulled with the fingers from the heart one leaf at a time. Dip each leaf in the accompanying sauce, place it in your mouth and pull it through your teeth scraping the meat off into your mouth. The remaining uneaten portion of the leaf is then placed on the plate on which the artichoke is served. The center of the artichoke is called the heart and is eaten with the knife and fork when the diner has finished eating the leaves. Eat this by cutting off the spiny feathers guarding the smooth gray heart. Cut the heart into small bites, and dip each bite into the sauce and enjoy.

Asparagus: Asparagus may be eaten with the fingers when they are firm. Place the portion of the asparagus that is too tough to eat on your plate. Eat asparagus cooked until limp with a fork.

Avocado: Eat with a spoon when served in its shell. Use a fork when filled with salad or presented as slices.

Bacon: Crisp bacon may be eaten with the fingers or with a knife and fork. Limp bacon is more easily eaten with a fork.

Baked Potatoes: Baked potatoes may be served wrapped in aluminum foil. Leave the foil on the potato to hold in the potato's heat and slit the foil open with your knife. Spoon condiments from serving dishes onto your plate and then onto the potato. You may add additional condiments as needed. Avoid stirring up the potato into a mashed mess.

Bouillabaisse: Bouillabaisse is a dish that includes seafood in a soup base. Eat with a soupspoon, fish fork and knife (or place fork, knife, and spoon if special utensils for eating fish are not available), and shellfish crackers when necessary.

Caviar: Caviar may be presented to you in an individual serving or on a passed serving dish. Cream cheese, diced hard-boiled eggs, finely chopped onions, capers, lemon wedges and small toast points, or crackers may accompany it. Use the knife to spread the cream cheese first and then the caviar and additional toppings as desired.

Celery, Olives, Relishes: These foods are generally served from a relish tray accompanied with a serving spoon or fork. Use the serving piece to place them on your plate. (Bread and butter plates may be used.) You may eat these foods with your fingers, from a toothpick, or with a fork.

However, be warned that spearing an olive can be difficult and there is danger in shooting it off your plate and into another diner's zone. Olive pits are removed from the mouth with the fingers then put on the bread and butter plate or the edge of the dinner plate.

Cherry Tomatoes: Cherry tomatoes are sometimes served on a relish tray and intended as a finger food. When utensils are not available, you must eat them in one bite to avoid squirting tomato juice. Cherry tomatoes in salad may be cut with knife and fork or eaten whole.

Dips: Cherry tomatoes and other raw vegetables, chips, etc. may be served with a dip. If a serving spoon is provided, spoon the dip onto your plate and dip your selections into the dip from your plate. It is rude to double dip directly into a communal dip bowl. Double dipping into a communal bowl is simply not healthy.

Corn on the Cob: Corn is generally served off the cob at formal dining events. Corn served on the cob may be cut off the cob by holding the cob at an angle and scraping the kernels off with a knife. People who have tight contacts between their teeth do this whenever they eat corn on the cob. For simple meals, corn may correctly be eaten off the cob. Butter and salt a few rows at a time. Hold the cob with both hands when eating.

French-Fries: Eat french-fries with your hands when you are eating informally. Cut fries into bite sized pieces using the side of the fork. Ketchup may be eaten with french-fries. Place the ketchup on the side of the plate and dip each bite into the sauce.

Fried Chicken: Fried chicken may be eaten correctly with the fingers or with a knife and fork. Generally, the setting will steer you in your choice. Picnics and fast food restaurants are typical places to eat fried chicken with the hands. Use utensils when a tablecloth is on the table.

Frog Legs: Frog legs are similar in taste and texture to fried chicken. The preferred way to eat frog legs is with a knife and fork, but it is correct to eat them with the fingers.

Gravy: Use the ladle in the gravy boat to put the gravy on your plate. Do not pour gravy from the boat.

Hors d'oeuvres served on a toothpick: Waiters may circulate serving a variety of hors d'oeuvres. Place the hors d'oeuvres on your cocktail plate or napkin. Do not eat directly from the serving tray and do not return the toothpick to the waiter's tray unless the waiter has a small plate or other receptacle for used toothpicks. Otherwise, once you have eaten food from a toothpick you must keep it on your plate or on your napkin until you find a suitable place to dispose of it. (Service table, wastebasket, etc.)

Lobster: Lobster is a messy food. The proper occasion to tie a napkin or bib around the neck is when eating lobster. Lobster requires the use of the hands, a cracker or mallet, and a cocktail fork. Once you have cracked open the shell, use your cocktail fork to pull the meat from the shell. You may cut large pieces into bite sizes with a knife and fork. Drawn butter is often served in individual dishes as a dip for lobster. Dip one bite of lobster at a time.

Peas: Peas are eaten with a fork. The European style is to use the knife to push the peas onto the fork. The American method is to push them onto the fork with a bit of bread held in the other hand.

Pizza: Eat pizza with you hand or cut it up one bite at a time with a knife and fork.

Sandwiches: Large sandwiches, triple decker sandwiches, and hot sandwiches are eaten with a knife and fork. Regular sized sandwiches are first cut in half with a knife and then eaten with the hands.

Shish Kebab: Remove the food from the skewer by holding it in one hand while using the other hand to slide off the meat with your fork. Cut food that is not easily eaten in one bite into a bite size before eating.

Soft Shelled Crabs: These crabs may be entirely eaten. Cut one bite at a time using a knife and fork.

Spare Ribs: Diners who hate to mess up their hands should avoid ribs. Many diners have tried to tackle ribs with utensils but eventually surrender to using their hands.

Stewed Fruit: Stewed fruit is most easily eaten with a spoon. Pits are removed from the mouth by discreetly spitting the pit into the spoon and back onto the plate or bowl.

Finger Foods

Pick up finger foods such as chips and nuts one item at a time. Use two fingers instead of greedily scooping a handful.

Some foods are perfect for eating with your hands. Foods that have a "handle" such as shrimp and firm asparagus may also be picked up with your fingers.

- *Pizza*
- *Sandwiches without gravy*
- *Hamburgers*
- *Hot Dogs*
- *Tortillas*
- *Artichokes*
- *Grapes*
- *Corn on the Cob*
- *Olives*

Sometime Finger Foods

- *Bacon when it is crisp*
- *Bananas when you are alone, but if it is sliced, eat it with a spoon or fruit fork*
- *French fries*
- *Fried chicken at picnics*
- *Watermelon when it is not served with utensils - usually outside or at a picnic*
- *Apples when you are alone or on a picnic. In a restaurant, cut and quarter apples.*
- *Celery. Break it in at least two pieces if it is long. Eat it with your hand. If you like salt, place some on your plate and dip the celery into it.*

How to Identify and Use Additional Silverware at the Table

Many formal restaurants have a retinue of silverware already in place when you are seated at the table. If you do not order specific foods, the waiter will remove unnecessary utensils. The types of spoons you may most often see are an iced teaspoon, a teaspoon, a pasta spoon, and a grapefruit spoon.

Types of Spoons

1. European Tablespoon
2. American Tablespoon
3. Teaspoon

4. Oval Soup
5. Round Soup
6. Sauce

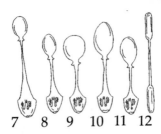

7. Iced Beverage
8. Five O'clock Teaspoon
9. Ice Cream

10. Melon or Grapefruit
11. Demitasse
12. Marrow

How to Hold a Spoon

Hold your spoon the same way you hold
a pencil.

Pasta Spoon

A pasta spoon is sometimes used for eating pasta. Debate
continues whether it is more elegant to grasp a few
strands of noodles with a fork and twirl them in the bowl
of a pasta spoon or to simply use the fork and the raised
rim of a pasta dish to accomplish twirling the pasta
around the fork's tines. In Italy, the choice of practice
varies from region to region. You may choose to mirror
your dining companion although most etiquette experts
agree that using the side of the plate to twirl the pasta is
neatest and most efficient.

Demitasse Spoon

Small spoons called demitasse spoons are used with
coffee served in small cups called demitasse cups. These
small spoons may also be used for serving condiments in
very small bowls.

Iced Teaspoon

The small-bowled and long handled spoon is the iced
teaspoon. As discussed earlier, stir your tea quietly,
remove the spoon from the glass, and place it on the
saucer under the glass or on another plate. (Never return
used utensils to the table). In addition for use with iced
drinks in tall glasses, it may be used for parfaits and as a
cocktail stirrer.

Berry Spoon

The berry spoon is a holdover from the Victorian period when expensive perishable berries were displayed in large elegant berry dishes as a symbol of wealth. Silver spoons could not be used with berries due to the acidic nature of fruit which causes silver to become pitted. Thus, a berry spoon, whose bowl is washed with gold, was designed for use with acidic fruits. Berry spoons are used today as an elegant alternative to modern stainless cutlery in any deep bowl containing acidic food.

Types of Forks

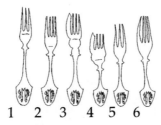

1. European dinner
2. American dinner
3. Fish

4. Salad
5. Steak
6. Luncheon

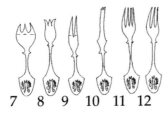

7. Oyster
8. Cocktail
9. Snail

10. Lobster
11. Dessert
12. Cake/Pastry

*   *The dinner fork, not the knife, is correctly used to put butter on vegetables and jellies on meats.*

Types of Knives

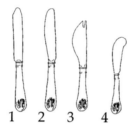

1. European dinner   3. Fish
2. American dinner   4. Butter spreader

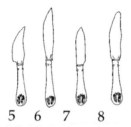

5. Butter server   7. Fruit
6. Steak   8. Luncheon

Silverware Dropped on the Floor

It is the duty of wait staff in a restaurant or private home to pick up dropped silverware from the floor. Pick up silverware from the floor yourself before help arrives if the utensil is in a hazardous position. Ask wait staff for a replacement. Pick up silverware from the floor if you drop it in someone's home and wait staff is not available. Ask the host for a replacement.

Wait Staff

The way you treat the wait staff indicates your respect for other people and of their time. A good restaurant will have an attentive staff, but even the best sometimes falters. If you need a waiter before one arrives on his own volition, do not snap your fingers or call out "waiter!" Summon help by catching the waiter's eye and slightly raise your brow and/or head. Raise your hand calmly if you fail to catch a busy waiter's attention with your eye.

Show respect for the waiter's time by requesting that he bring you whatever you want when he is back in the area. For example, "Please bring me some water when you return this way." Say, "thank you" for his effort. Wait staff have busy jobs and do not generally have time to engage in conversation. Further, it is not necessary to thank a waiter every time something is done for you, but it is welcome if you do recognize their service with a nod or smile of gratitude.

Serving

The waiter will serve the women before the men, beginning with the female guest of honor and proceeding counterclockwise around the table to the hostess, unless there is a second female guest of honor who would be served second. Men are then served in the same order beginning with the male guest of honor and concluding with the serving of the male host. All food is correctly served from the diner's left. All beverages are correctly served from the diner's right.

Plates may be served with the food on it, or the food may be passed and each diner will serve himself from a platter. The waiter will hold the platter for each person if wait staff is being used. If food is passed without the help of staff, the person seated on your left will hold the platter for you. The platter will circulate counterclockwise (to the right).

Side by side on the platter, with the handles facing you, will be a large serving spoon on the right (bowl up) and a large serving fork on the left (tines down). Take the fork in your left hand, tines down, and hold it in a steadying position. With your right hand, take the spoon, bowl up, and lift the food, using the fork to steady it.

After serving yourself, place the serving spoon and fork side by side on the platter, spoon on the right (bowl up) and fork on the left (tines down). In the absence of a waiter, you would next take the platter from the person to your left and then hold it for the person to your right.

It is not necessary to offer a serving to the person on your right before serving yourself. After a dish has been passed once around the table, the dish may be passed in either direction, taking the shortest route to the person who has requested it.

Salt and Pepper

Salt and pepper are positioned side by side with the pepper positioned to the left of the salt. (At a very formal table, every diner is likely to have an individual set of salt and pepper placed above his place setting.) Salt and pepper are always passed together and set on the table— not passed hand-to-hand. Never add seasoning to your food until you have tasted it.

Over the years, I have heard a particular salt story attributed to Henry Ford, J.C. Penney, and a past president of IBM. The story goes that the CEO would invite potential new hires out for a business meal to evaluate them. If the person being interviewed seasoned his food before tasting it, the CEO would not hire him. The CEO figured that the individual who does not test food before eating it would not properly examine products important to the company business. NEVER add seasoning to your food until you have tasted it.

Removing

Do not push the plate away from you to signal that you are finished or stack your plates in a heap to expedite efficient removal. Do place your silverware in the finished position to silently signal that you have completed eating the course. (As described earlier, this position is on the right side of the plate at the imagined four or five o'clock position. Note, in some cultures the finished position is indicated by placing the handles at the six o'clock position.)

It is easier for the waiter to remove dishes without handing plates to him. Your correct placement of the silverware in the finished position is a courtesy to the waiter as he can tidily grip underneath the plate with four fingers and place the thumb on the handles of your silverware to secure it while lifting it off the table.

If no staff is available, your host will remove the plates. You may offer to help if you are a close friend of the host, but if you are not, remain seated and out of the way.

Host Duties

The host's job is to be aware of the needs of his guests and to attend to those needs. When you are the host, ask your guests if they need anything. Notice when their drinks are empty, and if a waiter does not appear in due time it is correct to ask another waiter to offer assistance, or you can excuse yourself, find the manager, and ask for service. The guests respect this duty of the host and do not take over the host's duty.

Conversation at the Table

Pleasant conversation is expected at the table. It is not expected that anyone will dominate the conversation or serve as entertainment during the meal. It is expected that everyone will contribute to the conversation and listen to others.

At a large table where conversation with everyone is impossible, it is expected that each diner will spend equal time chatting with the person seated to either side of him. Avoid topics that may make others feel uncomfortable such as details of sickness, gory accidents, the cost of food or other items, gossip, religion, sex, and politics.

DINING SAVVY

Dining in a restaurant is a treat. No one in your family has to set the table or load the dishwasher. Eating in a restaurant is a great opportunity to visit with your family and eat different kinds of food that may not be served at home.

Some restaurants are more casual and serve familiar foods like hot dogs, hamburgers and pizza. Ethnic restaurants serve food familiar to a particular country such as Chinese, Indian, Mexican, Italian and Lebanese. Specialty restaurants serve certain types of food such as seafood or pizza.

Some restaurants are more formal. Such restaurants often use fancy starched linens and more flatware than you usually see at home. The people dining may be more dressed up and the atmosphere may be more quiet and reserved.

Restaurant Manners to Remember:

- Dress appropriately. Remember, neat and clean are always in style. At a fast-food restaurant almost any kind of clothing is acceptable. At nice, casual restaurants sweats or exercise clothes are not a good choice - but clean jeans and a tucked-in shirt might be okay. At formal restaurants jeans are not a good choice. Young men should wear khaki or corduroy pants and a shirt with a collar (and perhaps a jacket and tie.) Women should wear a skirt and blouse or sweater or a dress.

- Wait quietly to be seated.

- Remain in your seat when you are seated. If you see a friend, it's okay to smile and say hello - but do not visit his table. Visiting a table requires that the family members stop eating to talk. Standing by someone's table also creates an obstruction for the wait staff. If you need to visit the restroom you do not need to ask permission to leave the table. Say, "Excuse me," to those near you and leave quietly. Unless you are ill, one visit is all you should make.

- Don't touch anything on the table until the host/hostess picks up her napkin.

- Don't play with the flatware, the candle, and the sugar packets or salt and pepper shakers.

- Look at the menu carefully and choose food you will enjoy eating. Ask your host for a suggestion if you are not familiar with the food. (Your host's suggestion can also help you determine the price range of the food you order.)

- Keep the noise level at your table to a minimum. People sitting at other tables shouldn't be able to hear your conversation.

- Turn to the waiter, look him in the eye, and clearly give your order. Smile. Say, "May I please have the chicken supreme," not "I want the chicken thing."

- Don't eat too much bread or too many appetizers. Eat your bread by tearing off one bite at a time. Butter each bite. Save room for your meal.

- Say "please," and then "thank-you" when the waiter brings you something. Keep your conversation with the waiter to a minimum. The waiter is working and a prolonged conversation prevents him from serving you and other guests efficiently.

- Move slightly to the right as the waiter places your food in front of you.

- Sit up straight and properly in the chair with your feet in front of you. Dangling legs and chairs that are not pushed in properly can cause a waiter or another diner to trip and fall.

Grooming at the Table

Grooming does not take place at the table. Hands should not touch the face or head during the meal. Many women may have been taught that it is all right to reapply lipstick and a quick dab of powder at the social dining table. It is not attractive. If you need to repair makeup, excuse yourself from the table.

Use toothpicks in private.

Keep aftershave lotion and perfume faint so that a conversational partner would need to stand very close to smell any fragrance you are wearing.

Top Ten Tacky Table Offenders

Diners in a group often offend others at the table simply because they cannot see themselves as others do. Be aware that you unknowingly may have some personal habits that are repulsive. The top ten table offenders are listed.

1. Chewing food with an open mouth and forming it into a ball in one cheek. *(Chew small bites and do not chase your food with a beverage.)*

2. Talking with food in the mouth.

3. Making noise while eating such as smacking food, making cooing uumm...umm...sounds and crunching ice. *(Eat and chew as quietly as possible. Not only is the sound of crunching ice annoying, it can also crack the teeth.)*

4. Blowing the nose, coughing or sneezing at the table without covering the mouth. *(Excuse yourself from the table if you have time. If not, be sure to turn your head away from the table and use a handkerchief, not the napkin.)*

5. Asking for food without saying please and thank you.

6. Scratching and adjusting clothing at the table.

7. Talking about unappetizing or emotionally charged topics at the table.

8. Reaching across the table for food. *(Reach only for food that is within your personal space.)*

9. Gesturing with silverware.

10. Sopping food and pushing the plate away when finished.

When You Do and Don't Like the Looks of Your Food

- Try a small bite. You may be pleasantly surprised. If you don't like it, don't make a big deal out of it. Swallow it quickly and don't make a face event if it's a bug or a hair.

- Tell the waiter if you especially like your meal. He will tell the chef. Everyone likes to be complimented!

Problems at the Table

Awkward moments and bloopers at the table are inevitable and manifold including spilling food, drinks, burping, sneezing, and even passing gas. When I was growing up my father said, "If it can be spilled, Jane will spill it." Learning to deal with inevitable awkward moments at the table is important. Let's begin our discussion with my specialty, spilling, and discuss the best response to inevitable bloopers by the person committing the blooper, the host, and other guests who are present.

Neither the blooper nor the host should make a scene. Profuse apologies and displays of dismay extend the discomfort of both host and guests. Promptly tell your host if you spill and the accident is not noticed. This way the host or wait staff can clean it up. Guests who try to clean up the spill are often in the way and should therefore leave this responsibility to the host. Offer to have cleaned the carpet, chair, or table cloth you damaged. Follow up the next day and pick up the article for professional cleaning or arrange for a professional service to go to the home to repair the damage. Send flowers and a note to your host if he absolutely refuses to permit you to repair the damage. A graceful way for the host to make the guest feel comfortable in this situation is to keep right on talking when the spill occurs and as it is cleaned up. Not making a big deal out of the incident and acting nonchalantly will help the guest to save face. The host will be a hero to everyone who witnesses grace at the table. Guests who witness another guest's blooper should also behave in a nonchalant manner. From such small seeds of kindness grow fields of friendship.

Dropping utensils, food, and napkins can also make a person feel uncomfortable. The wait job in a restaurant includes picking up dropped items and replacing necessary items. Wait for your waiter to pick up what has been dropped unless it is in an area where someone may trip. Let your waiter know that you have dropped something if he does not notice. In a home where there is no wait staff, it is correct to pick up what has been dropped. Let your host know what your needs are. In homes in which you are as comfortable as an old shoe you can excuse yourself from the table and take care of your own needs!

Perhaps one of the most embarrassing things that can happen at the table is when a whoopee cushion is not present but the sound effects and odors are. Ugh. The person committing this is no doubt horrified and may not acknowledge his untimely natural biological function. If he says nothing, others present should remain silent and ignore the incident. Winks, laughs, and joking remarks are generally not well received. The offending guest may say, "Pardon me," "Excuse me, I am terribly sorry." Whatever he may choose to say should be extremely brief. Guests in this situation should overlook the incident and say little more than, "Think nothing of it. We all have that happen to us at sometime."

Dining equipment is not always clean. Discreetly inform the wait staff if you discover an unclean item at your place setting. Avoid embarrassing a host in a private home. If you choose to point the problem out to the host, be tactful and do not let other guests know of the problem. *Remember that you can eat later, but you cannot always repair a relationship damaged by a social blunder. Focus on conversation and building relationships.*

Food orders are not always served at the same time. Many find it awkward to let their food cool while waiting for others to be served. However, it is good manners to wait for everyone at a small table to be served before eating. At the small table, the guest who has been served has two correct options. First, he may elect to wait until everyone has been served before he begins to eat or he may request that the dish be returned to the kitchen to keep it warm until the others are served. Guests who have not been served may encourage the diner who has been served to begin eating. The only times I give in to this are when I am eating dishes which to me are inedible when cold - eggs and fish, or when other diners at the table send back their food for additional cooking or other reason. The etiquette of waiting for others to be served before eating is different at a large banqueting style table. At these tables, it is correct to begin eating when those in your immediate vicinity have been served.

Another awkward moment for diners arises when they discover something in their food that should not be there. Yikes! Every diner's appetite will be affected if the offensive stray hair, bug or whatnot is pointed out. Do not make a scene. Discreetly inform your waiter who will rectify the problem by removing the offending dish and offering a replacement. Dining in a private home is more delicate. Do not embarrass your host by pointing it out. Remember that you can eat later, but you can not always repair a relationship. Let your fork waltz around the food. Pick and move food around while you focus on conversation that is the true purpose of every dining event. This technique should also be used in a home when you are served a dish that you do not like.

Food does not always make it through the lips and into the stomach. Periodically wipe your mouth for stray food and run your tongue over your teeth. However, this technique is not foolproof and because diners do not look in mirrors when they eat they are liable to miss stray food. Who among us would not appreciate the favor of having our dining companion tell us what the rest of the world can observe about us that we cannot? Do your dining partner a favor by gesturing with your hand to the spot on your own face where the stray food is dangling or by politely saying something like, "Excuse me, you might want to know that there is some food on the side of your mouth."

Terrible food and poor service in a restaurant are hard to overlook. The host should apologize to his guest only once as laboring over unfortunate components of a communal gathering highlights the negative aspect of the occasion. Accentuating the positive aspects of dining is beneficial and desirable. The waiter or management should be privately informed by the host about the grossly negative parts of the dining experience in a restaurant. Do this at the restaurant *away* from the table or later with a telephone call or letter.

Leftovers, especially when they are good, are difficult to leave behind. However, it is not appropriate to take leftovers home with you from a very formal meal. Save the doggie bag for when you are dining with family and close friends.

Tipping

Good service is rewarded by the custom of tipping in the United States. It is not commonly practiced throughout the world so do familiarize yourself with local customs before doling out your money inappropriately.

Wait staff typically serve food, drinks, and answer menu questions. Wait staff in the United States are paid an amount lower than minimum wage so they expect tips of fifteen to twenty percent of the bill before taxes. A captain sometimes takes orders but does not serve. Captains expect a tip of five percent.

Bus boys are often hired to assist wait staff clear dishes, replenish coffee, tea, water, etc. They do not expect a tip from customers, but anticipate a share of the wait staff's tips.
Upscale restaurants may provide musicians. A pianist may have a bowl for tips. Strolling musicians may

circulate through the dining room and will gladly take any money handed them. Tips range from one to two dollars. You may tip more if you request special melodies.

Rest-room attendants may be available to hand you a towel or to offer grooming supplies. Tips range from one to two dollars when services are provided.

Door attendants and other people handling valet services may be tipped if they provide service to patrons. Door men are not tipped for opening doors but do expect a tip of about a dollar or two for hailing a cab — more in bad weather. Tip the same for parking service.

Taxi drivers taking you to and from your dining event expect a tip of ten to fifteen percent of the transportation fee.

CONCLUSION

Life requires respiration. Taking in and giving out. When you give of yourself you'll find that you get back more than you give. It is my hope that the formal rules, the etiquette, you learn will help you feel self-assured so that you can reach out to others and make them feel at ease for real happiness comes from not focusing on yourself but from thinking of others.

In closing, I'd like to share with you research that shows that in order for a skill to become a habit, it must be consistently practiced for twenty-one days or it will be forgotten. Use this book to remember what you have learned for lack of these skills even on the smallest level can damage your image and hinder you as you try to achieve social and career goals. Practice *The Etiquette Advantage*® life lessons you've learned until they are a part of your everyday storehouse of skills.

Good luck as you use *The Etiquette Advantage*® to help make your dreams come true. May comfortable communication with others be yours and may you be secure enough to have fun with many communication partners.

Jane Hight McMurry

BIBLIOGRAPHY

Adler, Ronald B. and George Rodman. *Understanding Human Communication.* Fortworth, Texas: Holt, Rinehart and Winston, Inc., 1991.

Ailes, Roger. *You Are The Message.* New York: Doubleday, 1998.

Axtell, Roger. Gestures: *The Do's and Taboos of Body Language Around the World.* Canada: John Wiley and Sons, Inc., 1991.

Baldridge, Letitia. *More Than Manners.* New York: Rawson Associates, 1997.

Ballare, Antonia and Angelique Lampros. *Behavior Smart!* West Nyack, New York: The Center for Applied Research in Education, 1994.

Basic Social Skills For Youth. Boys Town, Nebraska: The Boys Town Press, 1992.

Bell, Alice. *The Magic Power of Grooming in a Man's World.* Charleston, South Carolina: J & G Publishing Company, 1965.

Beyfus, Drusilla. *The You Guide To Modern Dilemmas.* London: Kyle Cathie Limited, 1996.

Bolton, Robert. *People Skills.* New York: Simon & Schuster, 1979.

Bone, Diane. *The Business of Listening.* Crisp Publications, 1988.

Bowman, Daria Price and Maureen LaMarca. *Writing Notes With A Personal Touch.* New York: Michael Friedman Publishing Group, 1998.

Brainard, Beth. *You Can't Sell Your Brother at the Garage Sale!* New York: Dell Publishing, 1992.

Brant, Madeline. *The Etiquette of Dress.* Sussex, England: Copper Beech Publishing Ltd., 1996.

Brinkman, Rick and Rick Kirschner. *Dealing With People You Can't Stand.* New York: McGraw Hill, 1994.

Dimitrius, Jo-Ellen and Mark Mazzarella. *Reading People.* New York: Random House, 1998.

Donaldson, Les. *Conversational Magic.* Paramus, New Jersey: Prentice Hall, 1981.

Dowd, Tom and Jeff Tierney. *Teaching Social Skills to Youth.* Boys Town, Nebraska: The Boys Town Press, 1992.

Duvall, Richard. *Character & Community.* Cypress, California: Creative Teaching Press, 1997.

Eichler, Lillian. *Today's Etiquette.* New York: Doubleday, Doran & Company, Inc., 1941.

Fitzgibbon, Theodora. *The Pleasures of the Table.* Oxford, England: Oxford University Press, 1981.

Frankel, Fred. *Good Friends Are Hard To Find.* Los Angeles: Perspective Publishing, 1996.

Freeman, Sara. *Character Education.* Grand Rapids, Michigan: Instructional Fair, 1997.

Gabor, Don. *How to Start a Conversation and Make Friends.* New York: Simon & Schuster, 1983.

Glass, Lillian. *Say It Right: How to Talk in Any Social or Business Situation.* New York: Perigee Books, 1992.

Goodwin, Gabrielle and David Macfarlane. *Writing Thank-You Notes.* New York: Sterling Publishing Co., Inc., 1998.

Gross, Kim Johnson and Jeff Stone. *Women's Wardrobe.* New York: Alfred A. Knopf, 1995.

Hall, Edward T. *The Silent Language.* New York: Doubleday, 1981.

Heatherley, Joyce Landorf. *Special Words.* Nashville, Tennessee: Moorings, 1996.

Herron, Ron and Val J. Peter. *A Good Friend: How To Make One, How To Be One.* Boys Town, Nebraska: Boys Town Press, 1998.

Hybels, Saundra and Richard L. Weaver. *Communicating Effectively.* New York: Random House, 1989.

Karns, Michelle. *How to Create Positive Relationships with Students.* Champaign, Illinois: Research Press, 1994.

Larkin, Jack. *The Reshaping of Everyday Life.* New York: Harper & Row, 1988.

Lavington, Camille. *You've Only Got Three Seconds.* New York: Doubleday, 1997.

Leaf, Munro. *Manners Can Be Fun.* New York: Harper & Row, Publishers, 1985.

Long, Sheila. *Never Drink Coffee From Your Saucer.* Kansas City, Missouri: Andrews and McMeel, 1996.

Maggio, Rosalie. *How to Say It.* Englewood Cliffs, New Jersey: Prentice Hall, 1990.

Maloff, Chalda and Susan Macduff Wood. *Business and Social Etiquette with Disabled People.* Springfield: Charles C. Thomas Publisher, 1988.

Martinet, Jeanne. *The Faux Pas Survival Guide.* New York: St. Martin s Press, 1996.

McCullough, Donald. *Say Please, Say Thank You.* New York: G.P. Putnam's Sons, 1998.

McMurry, Jane Hight. *The Dance Steps of Life*™. Wilmington, North Carolina: Stellar Publishing, 2001.

McGinnis, Alan Loy. *The Friendship Factor.* Minneapolis: Augsburg Publishing House, 1979.

Mole, John. *Mind Your Manners*. London: Nicholas Brealey Publishing Limited, 1996.

Morgan, John. *Debrett's New Guide To Etiquette & Modern Manners*. London: Headline Book Publishing, 1996.

Morganett, Rosemarie S. *Skills for Living*. Champaign, Illinois: Research Press, 1990.

Morris, Tom. *True Success*. New York: Berkley Books, 1995.

Nish, Steven Nish, ed. *Good Ideas to Help Young People Develop Good Character*. Marina Del Ray, California: Josephson Institute, 1998.

Nix, William H. *Character Works*. Nashville, Tennessee: Broadman & Holman Publishers, 1999.

Panati, Charles. *Panati's Extraordinary Origins of Everyday Things*. New York: Harper & Rowe, 1989.

Paston-Williams, Sara. *The Art of Dining*. London: National Trust Enterprises Limited, 1993.

Pierce, Beatrice. *It's More Fun When You Know the Rules*. New York: Rinehart & Company, Inc., 1935.

Pincus, Debbie and Richard J. Ward. *Citizenship*. Carthage, Illinois: Good Apple, 1991.

Post, Elizabeth L. *Emily Post on Guests and Hosts*. New York: Harper Perennial, 1995.

Prichard, Mari. *Guests & Hosts*. Oxford, England: Oxford University Press, 1981.

Ray, Veronica. *Choosing Happiness*. New York: Harper Collins Publishers, 1991.

Roberts, Patricia Easterbrook. *Table Settings, Entertaining, and Etiquette*. New York: Viking Press, 1967.

Roosevelt, Eleanor. *Eleanor Roosevelt's Book of Common Sense Etiquette*. New York: The Macmillan Company, 1962.

Ross, Pat. *The Pleasure of Your Company*. New York: Penguin Group, 1989.

Ross, Pat. *With Thanks & Appreciation*. New York: Viking Studio Books, 1989.

Sarnoff, Dorothy. *Never Be Nervous Again*. New York: Ivy Books, 1987.

Stewart, Donald Ogden. *Perfect Behavior*. New York: George H. Doran Company, 1922.

Stewart, Marjabelle Young and Ann Buchwald. *Stand Up, Shake Hands, Say "How Do you Do"*. New York: David McKay Company, 1977.

Stewart, Marjabelle Young. *The New Etiquette*. New York: St. Martin's Griffin, 1997.

Tannen, Deborah. *You Just Don't Understand*. New York: Ballantine Books, 1990.

Tannen, Deborah. *That's Not What I Meant!* New York: Ballantine Books, 1986.

The Art of Good Taste. Charleston, South Carolina: The Citadel® Print Shop, 1997.

The Etiquette of Politeness. Sussex, England: Copper Beech Publishing Ltd., 1995.

Tuleja, Tad. *Curious Customs.* New York: Harmony Books, 1987.

Van Fleet, James K. *Lifetime Conversation Guide.* Englewood Cliffs: Prentiss-Hall, Inc., 1984.

Villarosa, Riccardo and Giuliano Angeli. *The Elegant Man.* New York: Random House, 1990.

Visser, Margaret. *The Rituals of Dinner.* New York: Grove Weidenfeld, 1991.

Vogue's Book of Etiquette and Good Manners. New York: The Conde Nast Publications, Inc., 1969.

Washington, George. *Washington's Rules of Civility & Decent Behaviour In Company and Conversation.* Old Saybrook, Connecticut: Applewood Books, 1988.

Westmoreland, Rose. *Building Self-Esteem.* Torrance, California: Frank Schaffer Publication, Inc., 1994.

Wilson, Charles Reagan and William Ferris. *Encyclopedia of Southern Culture.* Chapel Hill, North Carolina: The University of North Carolina Press, 1989.

Wolfman, Peri and Charles Gold. *Forks, Knives & Spoons.* New York: Clarkson Potter/Publishers, 1994.

INDEX

ABOUT THE AUTHOR

Jane Hight McMurry

SociallySmart™ speaker, author, and trainer Jane Hight McMurry is the president of *SociallySmart*™and founder and managing director of **The Etiquette Advantage**® which provides training and support resources to help people achieve *SociallySmart*™ skills in communicating with people for professional and personal success. She is the author of *The Dance Steps of Life*™, *The Etiquette Advantage*®, *Readers Theatre for Senior Citizens,* and co-author of *Success is a Team Effort.* Jane speaks to audiences at all levels, from the frontline to the boardroom that want to achieve excellence in communicating with people.

Visit www.SociallySmart.com or telephone 910.762.0703 for more information about Jane Hight McMurry and the services of *Socially Smart*™ *and The Etiquette Advantage*®.

Quick Order Form

Please send the following books by Jane Hight McMurry.

QTY	ITEM	EACH	TOTAL
_____	**The Dance Steps of Life™**	$14.95	$_____
_____	**Success is a Team Effort**	$20.00	$_____
_____	**The Etiquette Advantage®**	$14.95	$_____
	SUBTOTAL		$_____

NC RESIDENTS ADD 6.5% SALES TAX $_____

POSTAGE AND HANDLING:
Add $2.00 one book + $ .90 more for each additional book.
CANADA: US Currency. ADD $3.00 for one book + $1.00
more for each additional book.

AMOUNT ENCLOSED $_____

<u>**FAX ORDER TO:**</u> 910-762-1766

<u>**MAIL ORDER TO:**</u>
Book Requests
PO Box 4544
Wilmington, NC 28406

<u>**SEND MY ORDER TO:**</u>

Name:

Address:

City: State: Zip:

Quick Order Form

Please send the following books by Jane Hight McMurry.

QTY	ITEM	EACH	TOTAL
_____	**The Dance Steps of Life™**	$14.95	$_____
_____	**Success is a Team Effort**	$20.00	$_____
_____	**The Etiquette Advantage®**	$14.95	$_____
	SUBTOTAL		$_____

NC RESIDENTS ADD 6.5% SALES TAX $_____

POSTAGE AND HANDLING:
Add $2.00 one book + $ .90 more for each additional book.
CANADA: US Currency. ADD $3.00 for one book + $1.00
more for each additional book.

AMOUNT ENCLOSED $_____

<u>**FAX ORDER TO:**</u> 910-762-1766

<u>**MAIL ORDER TO:**</u>
Book Requests
PO Box 4544
Wilmington, NC 28406

<u>**SEND MY ORDER TO:**</u>

Name:

Address:

City: State: Zip: